Art Is
Every Day

Art Is Every Day

Activities for the Home, Park, Museum, and City

Eileen S. Prince

Zephyr Press

Chicago

Copyright © 2012 by Eileen S. Prince
First edition
Published by Zephyr Press, an imprint of
Chicago Review Press, Incorporated
814 North Franklin Street
Chicago, Illinois 60610
ISBN 978-1-56976-715-3

Cover and interior design: Monica Baziuk
Front cover images: (*Clockwise from top left*) young girl sketching against a tree:
iStockphoto, © Mark Bowden; boy painting with watercolors: iStockphoto,
© Mlenny Photography; girl at a museum: iStockphoto, © Franky De Meyer;
watercolor brushstroke: Shutterstock, © Roman Sigaev; row of crayons:
Shutterstock, © Michal Vitek
Back cover and interior images: Author's collection

Library of Congress Cataloging-in-Publication Data
Prince, Eileen S., 1947–
    Art is every day : activities for the home, park, museum, and city /
    Eileen S. Prince.
          pages cm
      ISBN 978-1-56976-715-3 (pbk.)
    1. Art—Study and teaching (Elementary)—Activity programs. I. Title.
N350.P75 2012
702.8—dc23
                                                            2012005290

Printed in the United States of America
5 4 3 2 1

Contents

III At Home   29

IV At the Art Museum   93

Introduction

THE SEEDS OF this book were planted several years ago during discussions with a close friend. Her grandson is very talented in art. Every time I discussed some project we were doing in my class, she would say something like, "Oh, I wish my grandson went to your school. His art program is just awful!" Another friend's granddaughter is similarly gifted, but she has steadily lost interest, due in large part, I believe, to lackluster, empty art projects at her school. (As any educator will tell you, art programs are the first to feel the effects of a poor economy, and the recent focus on test results has exacerbated the problem. Trained art teachers are deemed expendable.)

The seeds were nurtured more recently by a somewhat different experience. A dear friend was planning to babysit her grandchildren for several days and asked if I had some simple art projects that might help pass the time in an enjoyable yet educational way. Since I was working on a book of lesson plans on that occasion, I easily picked a few that were appropriate.

Recent scientific and psychological discoveries about how the brain functions stress the importance of visual imagery to learning and memory. Such books as Daniel H. Pink's *A Whole New Mind* (Riverhead, 2006) suggest that the future will belong to people who develop those abilities associated with the right sides of their brains as well as those linked to the left. Spending time helping a child improve his or her creative and visual skills may have far-reaching benefits in later years.

There are several reasons you might use this book. You might be unhappy about your child's ineffective art program at school and wish to supplement it with substantive projects or discussions that will truly teach your child some basics. Or perhaps your child's school has cut its art program entirely due to budgetary constraints and you want to help fill the void. You might wish to keep your child interested in art until a time (usually high school) when he or she can take more productive courses. You might be pleased with your child's art program and merely wish to reinforce it. (Yes, there are some terrific art teachers out there!) Or you might be a teacher who would like to assign some enjoyable activities to support or enrich your program. You might want something fun yet educational to do during your child's or grandchild's vacation hours. Or you might want to start preparing your children for a future that relies heavily on so-called right-brained functions. You might not even *have* children—perhaps you want a few fun suggestions for projects that will whet your own appetite for further study!

The great thing about a valid art lesson is that it is self-individualizing. That is, given the same instructions, a kindergartener will complete the project at one level, a sixth grader at another, and an adult at still another. Most of the lessons I present here should be stimulating to people of any age.

Whatever your reasons for reading this book, please be aware that it is not a curriculum as such. If you are looking for a structured, step-by-step approach to art education, I encourage you to use my two previous books, *Art Is Fundamental: A Complete Guide to Teaching the Elements and Principles of Art in Elementary School* (Zephyr Press, 2008) and *Art Matters: Strategies, Ideas, and Activities to Strengthen Learning Across the Curriculum* (Zephyr Press, 2002). Together, those books can provide a complete curriculum for introducing art and art history to students. They present units in logical progression (see the "Social Studies" and "History" chapters in *Art Matters*), whereas the projects presented here follow no particular order. However, you can certainly use the activities in this book to supplement those volumes—to introduce or reinforce important concepts such as elements, principles, aesthetics, criticism, and art history. And, by using the "Index of Projects by Elements and Principles" included at the end, you could definitely arrange the activities in a more sequential way. (Note: If you have used either of my previous books, a few of these projects may seem familiar. However, in most cases, I have added to or changed some aspect of the activity, so don't assume the steps are identical.)

Many books on the market offer enjoyable projects—in fact, I urge you to try some. What sets this book apart, I believe, is the fact that it presents vocabulary and concepts as well as hands-on exercises, and it includes conceptual, intellectual projects as well as physical ones. But once again, this is not intended to be a complete curriculum.

It is not necessary for you to be familiar with the vocabulary involved or to have any special skills before you start. In fact, if you are a parent or grandparent, studying the material with the child could be a terrific lesson in itself. Think of the great example you will set as a lifelong learner. It would, however, be an excellent idea to read this entire introduction and the vocabulary overview on pages 3–16 before you begin. If an activity seems fraught with potential pitfalls, you might want to try it before "teaching" it, but most of the ideas I have included are pretty easy. I have also tried to avoid lots of exotic, expensive materials, although you might want to invest in a couple of special media if your child seems particularly interested or involved. But let me stress that the fundamentals of art are principles such as composition and color theory, and these concepts can be well taught with surprisingly simple supplies.

One of the main purposes of the activities in this book is to help the participant to "see." We look at so many things in the world around us without actually registering the details of those subjects—their shapes, textures, lines, forms, and colors—that we can sometimes be surprised by their beauty and complexity. The most common object, when truly seen, can provide an aesthetic opportunity. Learning to appreciate beauty in the world around us can be a wonderful experience.

This volume should be fairly easy to use. It is divided into different sections based on the type of environment in which you might find yourself. Several of the activities or projects are appropriate for more than one location, and one idea or experience might inspire you to do something similar but not identical, so it might be a good idea to read through the entire book before starting. But that's not absolutely necessary. Whether you are using this book for yourself, your students, your children, or your grandchildren, I hope you enjoy it!

What Is Art and Why Should We Study It?

What *is* art? Any teacher who has ever introduced students to the vast range of 20th-century works has grappled with that question. Even artifacts as ancient as Egyptian mummies raise significant questions about the choices we make for our "art" museums. Is a *modern* coffin "art"? When is it OK to dig up Aunt Tillie and put her on display? When does her tomb become "art"? After ten years? One hundred? Is a quilt that follows a pattern "art"? Do my first graders do "art" in the same sense that Michelangelo did it? How do we teach something if we don't really know what it is to begin with? *Why* should we teach it?

I teach art in first grade through eighth grade. In first grade, second grade, and third grade, my units center around the elements and principles of design and the development of vocabulary. Students learn about geometric and organic shapes; color theory; symmetrical, radial, and informal balance; and many other concepts. In fourth grade through seventh grade, the curriculum focuses on art history and theory. Eighth grade is a time for students to draw upon all of this background and begin to develop a personal style. Throughout the years, assignments and projects are treated as visual problems to be solved, and while I always insist that my students create their own solutions to these tasks, in eighth grade the problems themselves become intensely personal as well, involving a great deal of self-portraiture and introspection. And though we are always dealing with questions of aesthetics and learning critical skills, our first unit in eighth grade focuses specifically on these two concepts. In fact, the entire year's curriculum requires the students to explore their beliefs about the nature of art.

I have struggled with the definition of art throughout my many years of teaching, and I have never found a statement that seems to work all the time for every situation. In my first book, *Art Matters*, I discuss several approaches that I like. My favorite so far can be found in Richard L. Anderson's wonderful book, *Calliope's Sisters* (Pearson, 2004). He concludes that art is "culturally significant content, skillfully encoded in an affective, sensuous medium." A simpler version of this sentiment can be found in the book *After the End of Art* (Princeton, 1998), where Arthur C. Danto paraphrases Hegel by saying that "art is about something, and it has a vehicle." (The "vehicle" is the medium: the play, the song, the painting, the dance.) Professor Marcia Eaton frequently states that one quality necessary to an artwork is that it must "repay sustained attention." In eighth grade we discuss these and other concepts at length. A few examples of current thinking include "It's art if the artist says it's art," "It's art if the viewer says it's art," and "It's art if it's in a museum or gallery." Needless to say, I have some issues with each of these statements.

All of the above, however, was of little help when one of my first graders asked me for my definition of art. First grade had just conducted its annual Communications Fair, and Sara's presentation had been on art. After she finished, her teacher suggested that she ask me my definition and compare it to the one she had used for her project. Now, I don't believe in talking down to children or patronizing them, but Anderson's quote was simply not going to be of much use in such a situation. So I fell back on a concept that I also discuss briefly in my books, the idea of art as a unique language.

"Art," I said, "is a way we can communicate without words (although I qualified my statement by pointing out that some artists use words in their art). I may weave or paint or sculpt or build to tell you a story, describe how someone looks, or express my emotions. I might 'tell' you about a color or shape or call your attention to the beauty of a leaf."

We discussed different things that artists want to "say" and different ways to say them. Then I quoted a local artist who told one of my eighth graders, "Art is the way I introduce myself before I meet someone."

This quote is the result of a project we do in eighth grade. Each student is required to visit a gallery or an art fair, select one of the works he or she encounters, contact the artist, and ask that person a series of questions. I recommend that they choose from local artists, and indeed, some students are able to visit their artists' studios. Others correspond with the subject by e-mail or phone. One of the questions on the list is "What is your definition of art?" Answers range from artist centered to viewer centered and from specific to vague, but most relate to my answer to Sara's question. And, at least for purposes of art criticism, the idea of art as a form of conversation may help students ultimately decide on the nature and merit of a work, and it might offer a practical way to discuss aesthetics with your student or child.

There is nothing new about the concept of art as visual communication. Elliot Eisner speaks of art as an alternative way of knowing the world, and most art teachers explore the many ways in which artists can express themselves and understand what other artists are saying. I have always stressed to my classes my personal conviction that art is indeed a form of communication, and that communication is a two-way street, requiring both a speaker and someone to listen. If I speak and no one hears or understands me, I have not communicated anything (although you might argue that I am talking to *myself*). However, I never really expanded on the idea as a way to help students understand the many approaches and degrees of success an artist may have in creating a work; I never developed the concept to illuminate the difference between what Daniel Pinkwater refers to—in his book *Fish Whistle* (Addison-Wesley, 1990)—as "Big A" Art and "little a" art. Using the analogy between visual art and verbal communication can be enormously helpful in many ways.

It seems to me that the most valuable form of communication is when a speaker says something profound that causes me to think deeply about the statement or concept or that expands my general knowledge or understanding. (Conversely, we all know people who talk endlessly and actually say little or nothing.) Perhaps the speaker is saying something profound, but I have a headache, or I don't hear her clearly, or I simply don't care about the topic. *Perhaps I don't understand the language being spoken.* Maybe the speaker is discussing a subject that is extremely important to people living in Alaska but seems irrelevant to a person from Indiana. Some conversations seem vitally important at the moment they are taking place but they are forgotten a week later, while some statements are so insightful they become quotations, repeated for centuries. Perhaps a remark by someone seems trivial at the time but turns out later to have contained profound import. A discussion may be pleasant but not profound, and we remember it fondly: "I had such a lovely visit with so-and-so yesterday. He says the nicest things!" I mentally revisit the experience and enjoy repeating the encounter whenever "so-and-so" and I chance to meet, but the result is not life changing. Some sentiments are so moving and couched in such beautiful language they create an unforgettable experience. Perhaps there is a great deal of symbolism. Some people simply repeat what others have said and never offer an original thought. Some people are patently insincere in their utterances. Some are witty or whimsical or satirical. Perhaps I totally misunderstand what the speaker is saying! The similarities between verbal and visual conversations are almost endless.

When discussing the definition of art with my eighth graders, I frequently refer to the saying "If everything is art, nothing is art." Teachers who deal with this age level are probably familiar with the tendency of such students to rank virtually anything as art, and studying what is going on in the contemporary art world only reinforces that attitude. Even though my students are fully aware that beauty is not a necessary quality in an artwork, many of them will nonetheless allow a nice aesthetic to override other considerations. Thus a glorious sunrise, a majestic mountain, or a lovely seashell may be considered art.

I try to make very few definitive pronouncements in our study, preferring that my pupils explore several possibilities and craft one that works for them. However, I do require that the definition include the concept of a maker other than a supreme being. Depending upon your belief system, God may speak to you through the beauty and wonders of the world, but for art class we are seeking a more secular and limited meaning. I am no philosopher, but I have never read a scholarly definition of art that did not include or imply a human component. I may be moved by the beauty of a seashell as it lies on the beach, but it does not become a work of art until there is some sort of human intervention. I may very well find inspiration in the shell, but unless I pass my thoughts along to someone else, I am simply talking to myself. My students learn a great deal about math, science, social studies, history, language arts, and performing arts from my curriculum, but if there are no limits to what qualifies as art, then the administration had better give me a lot more class time.

One dilemma that may be resolved by the analogy between art and conversation is the question of artifacts that appear in art museums but were not intended to be art when they were created. A prehistoric pot, however aesthetically pleasing, was probably created for use, not as a work of art in the sense we use that term. The paintings on the walls of an Egyptian tomb were intended to persuade the gods that the deceased was worthy of eternal life and to beautify the environment in which his or her *ka* would spend that eternity. They were certainly not painted in order to be discussed several thousand years later by visitors touring the premises. So why are they art now?

If we continue our analogy, such artifacts become art when they communicate with us, as they most certainly do. The potter and the tomb painter both used the vocabulary of their cultures in their creations. Their products now tell us an enormous amount about the culture of the period and place they represent. A certain aesthetic quality, visual form, and uniqueness are necessary to fully qualify the work as art. What Anderson calls "skillful encoding in an affective, sensuous medium," and what Dantos (via Hegel) calls "the vehicle," is one half of the equation, but it is not the whole story. The "significant cultural content"—the "aboutness"—is equally important and may not happen while ancient artifacts are in their own milieu. Years later, however, they may tell quite a tale or communicate a vast amount of information. Somebody (I wish I knew who!) said, "Art is what lasts. In fact, if it lasts, then it is art." And while people at any given point on the time line might choose differently, what we study in art history classes today is, essentially, the stuff that has lasted.

The analogy also makes a strong case for the importance of art education. If art is a purely emotional response to a perceived visual image, or the purely emotional, instinctive creation of that image, then there is little that I as an art teacher have to offer. Different people will simply "draw what they feel" or react differently to different stimuli by virtue of their personalities and preferences. I might cause a student to appreciate the difficulties inherent in a process or draw attention to works in a way that allows the class to see more than they might otherwise have done—and I certainly make every effort to do so—but students wouldn't really need much elaboration.

But if art is truly communication, then it is vitally important that the communicating parties speak the same language. While I may get the gist of what someone is saying in Mandarin through universal gestures, body language, tone, and so forth, unless I speak—or at least understand—Mandarin, I'm going to miss most of the message. Art may be a *universal* language, but it is a language nonetheless. As with any language, the more one understands its vocabulary, structure, and nuance, the better one may communicate. Art-educated students are able to express themselves more fluently and are more capable of understanding what other artists are trying to say. For some students, the visual arts may be their "mother tongue," offering the most viable means of self-expression.

We live in an era when many believe "high" art is becoming increasingly difficult for the average person to comprehend. While we may have unrestricted right of entry to museums and galleries, our fundamental access to these venues is limited by our ability to relate to the art we find there. (Some might liken today's art scene to a veritable Tower of Babel, with so many artistic "languages" being spoken that it is necessary to learn a multitude of them.) At the same time, "low" or commercial art permeates every facet of our lives. One way or another, we are constantly being addressed in the language of art, and if we fail to study that language, we are going to miss a lot of information.

The study of art, like the study of any language, involves learning vocabulary and syntax, idiom and nuance. One should try to think in the language, to immerse oneself in a society that speaks that native tongue. Different cultures may interpret words differently, and language changes over time. The more fluent we become in the language of art, the more it can tell us about society, about our world, about history, and, most important perhaps, about ourselves.

We live in a society that is relying ever more heavily on visual communication. It is essential that our children become "bilingual," not only to understand the stories of the past but to fully understand the messages of the present. In the babble of modern tongues, art is a unifying language. Learning that language helps us understand, appreciate, and respect elements that are unique or similar among various cultures, whether those cultures be American or Australian, modern or medieval, gay or straight, black or white, young or old. And the better we understand those other cultures, the more likely it is that we will find that all of us, no matter how disparate we may seem, share certain fundamental human qualities far more important than the issues that divide us.

What Is a Substantive Art Program?

There is still a certain amount of disagreement as to what constitutes a great art program. I am a fan of structured curricula that reflect tenets of discipline-based art education (DBAE)—that is, programs that contain elements of art history, art criticism, aesthetics, and production. While I incorporate these aspects differently than the Getty Foundation model, my curriculum does cover all these areas. I strongly believe in incorporating science, math, language arts, history, social studies, and music into my classes, and I focus a great deal on developing vocabulary. Some art teachers disagree with such a curriculum as being *too* structured. They favor a more experimental, "creative" approach, with less direction and more freedom. I am sure that their students have a lot of fun and produce some terrific work, but I feel it is my job to teach as many of the fundamentals as possible in the time allowed. I would contend that my students also have a lot of fun and that they lose not one jot of their creativity. In fact, I would argue that their creativity is enhanced by understanding the possibilities and having the skill to translate their visions into reality.

As I stated in *Art Matters*:

Art has never been a purely visual exercise. While my response to a work may be intensely aesthetic, it will always involve an emotional or intellectual component. Perhaps the best art will engage me on all three levels. From the creator's point of view, art requires constant decision making, no matter how subconscious those decisions might be. Michelangelo recognized the intellectual component of art when he wrote "A man paints with his brains and not with his hands." ...

[In my opinion,] a valid art curriculum presents significant content and continuously develops the students' problem-solving skills. It requires constant decision making on the part of the pupils, demands high standards of achievement, and instills in the students a deep respect for art as a discipline. It accommodates all learning styles and is self-individualizing. It promotes intellectual honesty and curiosity, and it encourages diversity. It discourages judgments based upon ignorance and prejudice. It honors excellence. I believe that the content and methodology found in a quality art class are parallel to the substance and structure of any other well-taught discipline.

Perhaps the best way to describe my ideal curriculum is to explain what the product of such a program can do. I would like to think my students have certain basic skills in drawing, sculpting, and painting. They understand perspective and human proportions. They have a large vocabulary of elements and principles and can describe what they see in an artwork appropriately. In fact, they see more because they have studied this vocabulary. They have a basic sense of successful composition.

When viewing a work of art, they have a good idea of what the artist was trying to achieve. They recognize certain periods and styles. They are able to look critically at a work of art. They are able to express themselves visually. They believe art is an important part of our culture.

Do I truly believe *all* my students have *all* these abilities and attitudes? Of course not. But that is the type of pupil I am trying to develop, and some of my students come pretty close!

Critiquing

The projects in this book are designed to be both fun and educational. If we were using them in a school setting, the students and I would be critiquing the products throughout their creation. In fact, one of the tacit lessons I teach is the importance of constant self-examination. Does my craftsmanship reflect my best effort? Is my composition balanced? Does the work communicate my intended meaning? A good critique conveys both the positive and negative answers to these questions. (We use the term in the sense of "assessment" or "appraisal.") "I love the way you have drawn the pony in your picture, but I feel you need something else to fill this large negative space." If you are an art teacher using these lessons to supplement your program, you will find several ways to incorporate critiques, but if you are someone with little or no art background, it might be difficult for you to make observations that help the child improve his or her work. And, of course, you won't be leading a class as such, so the tenor will be more relaxed anyway.

However, I still think you can set a certain tone. Even if you are only doing an occasional project from the book when the grandkids visit, you can take the product seriously, and that might help the child think more critically about the work. By "seriously," I mean looking at the work in the same way you would a piece in a museum. Don't automatically nod and tell the child how wonderful it is. Give it a careful perusal, *then* tell Janey how great her project is. If you note something, you might mention it. "I love the way you drew the tree, John. Maybe next time you could make it a bit bigger so we can see it better." Or "I really like it. What do you think of it? Artists are always very critical of their own work, so I wondered if you were happy with it." You might ask if he or she would change anything or do anything differently the next time. You might be surprised that what looks wonderful to you is disappointing to the artist. I can't count the times a student working on a piece I find terrific has asked if she can start over.

You want to be encouraging, of course, but not patronizing. Children frequently know they are having problems with their work, and if you fail to notice, you may well lose credibility. Also, the "It's only an art project, anything you do is acceptable" attitude is hardly likely to foster respect for art or the artist. So a nice blend of approval with an occasional suggestion or gently couched critical remark should indicate you respect the child enough to take him seriously but generally like the work. While you may not be an art teacher as such, I hope you will consider the following point of view about art education I expressed in *Art Is Fundamental*:

> We hear a great deal in today's culture about "self-esteem," and teachers are taught that one of the most important aspects of affective education is the development of the student's feeling of self-worth. While I am totally in agreement with this sentiment, I think many parents and teachers are laboring under a misconception about how to help children improve this facet of their personalities, and this misconception has had an almost disastrous effect on art education. Because so many people view art class, at least at the elementary level, simply as a therapy/play period without significant content or standards, they feel it is a good place to praise virtually anything a student produces without regard to true merit. Art teachers are frequently advised to refrain from judging student work, on the theory, I suppose, that suggesting something needs improvement might be damaging to the pupil's self-esteem. Imagine this theory being applied to piano lessons or math homework. I believe this is a self-defeating practice on many levels.

In the first place, you cannot "confer" self-esteem on someone simply by telling them how wonderful they are if they see no personal evidence to support your assertion. A pupil who rarely solves a math problem correctly is not going to believe that he is a terrific math student no matter how many times you tell him that he is. We might fairly laud his effort and work ethic but not his product. And while I suppose that a child bombarded from birth with protestations of her wonderfulness might come to believe it after a while, what real service does that do her? Of course I believe in general praise that offers the child acceptance as a human worthy of respect, and naturally I do not advocate belittling or denigrating remarks. But true feelings of self-worth come when we meet and overcome obstacles.

Second, children are not stupid. They know when they are being patronized. "Dumbing-down" the curriculum only denies them skills they will need in later life without providing the self-esteem boost such an action is theoretically designed to supply, and simply offering indiscriminate praise is just as bad. If two of my students are trying to draw a horse realistically, and one child's work looks like a Kentucky Derby winner while the other resembles a lobster, I am not going to tell the lobster artist how wonderful her drawing is. Even the slowest child knows the difference between a horse and a lobster. Not only will my false praise do nothing to help the child achieve her goal, but it will cause me to lose all credibility with her, and any legitimate praise I may offer later will be meaningless. My job is to help her draw a horse of which she can be justifiably proud. So while developing self-esteem might be high on my list of affective results achieved through art, the way I would accomplish that end is by presenting challenging projects and teaching my students that they can achieve pretty much anything with proper instruction and hard work.

Of course, most of the people using this book may not be classroom art teachers, but I believe the general philosophy stated above is still pertinent. Be honest in your comments, but certainly try to find the things you can *honestly* praise.

If you feel your child's work is extraordinary in some way, but you don't feel qualified to judge its artistic merit, take it to a professional. If you are happy with your child's art teacher, share the work with that individual, but if you aren't (or, as is more likely, there isn't one), seek out someone at another school or perhaps a local university.

Portfolios

Many teachers keep portfolios of student work. Even if you are working at home with your child or grandchild, it would be an excellent idea to have a box or file folder where you can store some of the finished projects. It's amazing what you can tell about a youngster's progress by looking at his or her work over a period of time. If nothing else, you can judge the development of small muscle coordination.

One of my least favorite synonyms for creativity is the phrase "coloring outside the lines." In my experience with young children, coloring outside the lines rarely has much to do with creativity. It is usually a reflection of haste, lack of effort, or poor motor skills. Every artist must be able to color inside the lines when necessary. The trick is to know when it's not necessary. Some projects look better when done in a free, exuberant style, but some just look messy. One of the benefits of art classes is to help children focus on craftsmanship, which is usually a reflection of muscle development and effort. A portfolio can tell you a great deal about such issues.

Another result of keeping a portfolio is the message it sends to the child. It implies that her work is important. That *art* is important. If you are a parent, this probably won't be a problem, but if you are a grandparent or noncustodial parent—someone who lives in a different location—it might present some difficulties. Perhaps you could encourage the child to do a duplicate project occasionally: one for himself and one for you. The easiest way to solve this problem is to take a photo of the finished piece, print it on plain paper, and file the print in the child's portfolio.

Materials

In this book, I have tried to avoid projects that require expensive or hard-to-find materials. When something like a camera is required, I have tried to provide alternatives. However, you will find it easier to use this volume if you have some basic supplies. A pencil, an eraser, and paper are absolutely necessary, as are scissors and glue. For most of the projects, glue in stick form is the best idea. Crayons are fairly essential. Crayola's box of 24 will work well, but if you want a larger set, that's fine. A box of markers will be helpful, preferably the washable variety. Certain projects require very specific supplies, like food coloring or plaster of paris, but several require no materials at all.

The one tool that I strongly recommend is a digital camera. If you don't own one, perhaps a friend or relative has a camera you could borrow. The same applies to a printer. You are better off with a regular printer, which uses 8½-by-11-inch plain paper, than with a photo printer. While not absolutely necessary, these devices will make some of the projects far more effective. (If you can print your photos from your cell-phone camera, that's fine, too.)

Art Is
Every Day

I

A Brief Overview of Elements, Principles, and Other Terms

1. Elements

The term "elements" refers to the various basics that go together to create a work of art: color, value, texture, shape, form, and line. Some artists add "space" to this list, but I discuss space in terms of shape and form.

Color

The way light is reflected, absorbed, or refracted by pigmentation, liquids, or atmosphere.

Believe it or not, even first graders can comprehend the nature of color if it is presented properly. (See *Art Is Fundamental* for an introduction to color.) Basically, color refers to how we perceive light and its different wavelengths. Our perception of color depends on the light source. You have probably noticed that incandescent bulbs emit a glow that looks different from that cast by fluorescent ones. We call the light from our sun white light, because it contains all the colors of the rainbow mixed together. White light looks clear until it is reflected or refracted.

A little lesson in optics is called for here. (Don't worry—this is actually fun!) When white light strikes a surface, several things may happen. In some cases, none of the light is absorbed into the surface. It all bounces back and strikes our eyes. When this happens, we see that surface as white. If all the light is absorbed, nothing bounces back to hit our eyes. We call the absence of light black. (We will discuss black and white at greater length in the section on value.) Pigments in the surface are responsible for what we see.

Some pigments allow every color of the rainbow to be absorbed except for red. When light strikes an object with such a pigment, only the red bounces back to our eye, and we see the object as red. If I put such an object in a room with only a green bulb, the object will appear black, because there is no red light to bounce back to our eyes. Understanding how light affects color can save you a lot of money when choosing carpets, fabrics, and wallpaper!

The primary colors of pigment are red, yellow, and blue. They are capable of creating all other colors, but no other colors can mix to make them. Two primary colors mixed somewhat evenly will create a secondary color. Yellow and blue make green, yellow and red make orange, and red and blue make purple. (This is a generalization. A lot depends on whether you are using warm or cool primaries, but that is a bit more advanced concept, and it is not necessary to go into it at length here.) If two primaries are mixed unevenly, they create intermediates. Lots of yellow and a little red will make a yellow-orange. Lots of red and a little yellow will make a red-orange. If you mix two secondaries, you will get a tertiary. Tertiaries are rather odd, dull colors like slate (green and purple), russet (orange and purple), and bronze (orange and green).*

*When I was a young art student, there was a distinct difference between the definitions for "intermediate" and "tertiary." As stated above, an intermediate color is made by mixing uneven amounts of two primary colors. A tertiary is made by mixing two secondaries. The results are totally different. Now, granted, I have not been a young art student for a long time, but the results are still totally different. Intermediates are bright, pure colors. Tertiaries are dull colors. Now many websites and other sources define them interchangeably. They will tell you that the term "tertiary" can refer to a color made by mixing two secondaries, or it can be another word for an intermediate. How is this possible? The results are totally different! If you discuss this vocabulary, I urge you to use the true definitions of these terms. A nice summary of color definitions appears at www.woodfinishsupply.com/ColorTheory.html.

A Brief Overview of Elements, Principles, and Other Terms

Neutral colors are those that don't appear on a color wheel, things such as beiges and browns. Browns can be made in different ways, but one way is to mix all three primaries together somewhat evenly. We usually refer to greens, blues, and purples as cool colors and yellows, reds, and oranges as warm colors.

Colors can be described in three ways—by hue, value, and intensity. We call these the three properties of color.

Hue is simply the name of the color. Blue is a different hue from blue-green.

Value refers to how light or dark the color is. A purple crayon right out of the box is darker than a yellow one. I can lighten a color by adding white. A color with white added is called a tint. I can darken a color by adding black. A color with black added is called a shade.

Intensity refers to how bright or dull the color is—its purity. Certainly, changing the value of a color will change its intensity, but I can have two colors with the same value and one can be very bright while the other is very dull. I can dull a color without changing its value by adding gray. Artists frequently dull colors by mixing in a touch of the color opposite on the color wheel. (See complementary color scheme below.) A dull version of a color is called a tone.

Color schemes are deliberate plans of (usually) harmonious colors chosen by the artist. If you check the color wheel in the color-insert section, page C-1, you will see certain relationships. You can add black, white, or gray to any color scheme without altering it in any way, and you may use different values and intensities of the chosen hues. (Actually, color schemes are rarely "pure." We use the term to refer to the predominant colors used in an artwork, interior design, clothing, and many other things.)

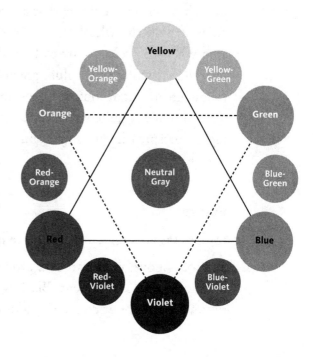

A monochromatic color scheme uses only one color from the wheel and its various tints, shades, and tones.

A complementary color scheme uses two colors that lie opposite each other on the color wheel. Complementary colors are fascinating. If you stare at an area of color for 25 to 30 seconds and then look at white for a bit, you will see an afterimage of the area in the opposite, or complementary, color. (I have included an activity for this, "Staring at Colors," on page 53.) Complementary colors placed side by side intensify each other—they make each other appear brighter. But if you mix a bit of a color into a large amount of its opposite, it will dull that color.

If you mix two opposites somewhat evenly, you will get gray or black. (This only works if the colors are truly opposite. The yellow in a box of Crayola markers is not the opposite of the purple in that same box, nor are the blue and orange exact complements, but the red and green work fairly well.)

A triadic color scheme uses any three colors that lie equally far apart on the color wheel. Primaries are always triadic, as are secondaries, but for a truly triadic arrangement using intermediates, you should use a wheel with 18 colors.

An analogous color scheme involves a group of colors that lie next to each other on the wheel that are related in some way. You can start anywhere on the wheel and go in either direction, but you have to stop when the colors start to be opposite. Thus, I might use purple, blue-violet, violet-blue, blue, green-blue, blue-green, and green, but yellow-green might look a bit too much like purple's opposite. Once again, no one is quite so picky about such things, but when I'm teaching a concept, I like to stay as pure as possible so that I don't confuse the students.

Value

The way the artist uses light or dark in a work of art.

As noted above, value can be a property of color, but it can also stand alone as a separate element. Black, white, and grays by themselves are pure values without color. Without different values, it would be very hard to see. Think about reading a book printed with gray ink on light blue pages! Using different values creates visibility.

Texture

The way something feels or the way it appears to feel—its surface quality.

Artists use texture in several ways. Sculptures, collages, and buildings, for instance, display *real* textures as themselves. The parts that look rough are rough, the parts that look smooth are smooth. Painters frequently create the *illusion* of texture. While the picture may depict velvet and satin and lace and hair, the painting itself may be totally glossy. Other artists focus on the texture of the *materials* they are using—the paint, the wood, the tessera—regardless of the subject matter. If you look at the painting *Starry Night* by Vincent van Gogh, the first thing you will notice is the texture of the paint itself.

Shape

A two-dimensional—or flat—closed figure.

Technically, for mathematical purposes, a shape has only length and width, no depth. For artistic purposes, the word "flat" is close enough. We would refer to a canvas as a two-dimensional medium, even though it is technically a form.

Shapes with names and rules are referred to as geometric shapes. If I say "square" to a group of people, everyone will picture a figure with four equal sides and four 90-degree corners. If I say "cloud" or "blob," the possible images are endless.

Figures without names or rules might be organic or irregular. Organic shapes tend to look like living things—think of an amoeba—while irregular shapes are more angular. A bolt of lightning is one example of an irregular shape. An artwork composed of only geometric shapes will look quite different from one that uses only organic figures.

When I draw a shape on a blank canvas, the shape that I draw is referred to as a positive shape. The background shape that is created at the same time is called the negative space. In a good composition, the artist will consider the negative space as carefully as the positive space. Imagine two drawings of a person. In one drawing, the person fills the entire page—there is very little negative space around him. Now imagine exactly the same figure, but it is quite small in the center of the page, with a great deal of negative space. The effects of these pictures will be very different. The first picture might give us a feeling of being caged or trapped, while the second might impress us with a sense of loneliness or isolation. Sometimes children like to draw things very small. Depending upon the purpose of the piece, it is frequently a good idea to encourage them to enlarge the positive shapes.

If an image consists of only positive shapes, we refer to the design as tessellated.

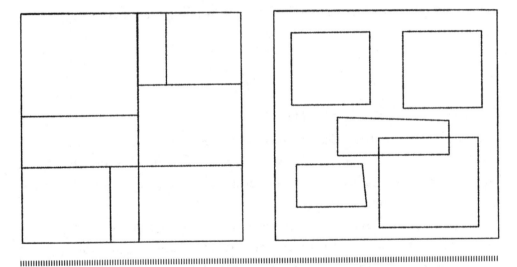

The image on the left is tessellated; the one on the right is not.

Form

A three-dimensional, closed figure.

A form encloses volume. Like shapes, forms can be geometric, organic, or irregular. Cubes, cones, cylinders, and daisies are all forms.

Some artists use shading (changes in values) to create the illusion of form on a two-dimensional surface. Others, like potters and sculptors, create actual forms. The idea of positive and negative space that was discussed in the explanation of shape can be applied to form as well.

Line

The path of a moving point.

In mathematics, line refers to an infinite, one-dimensional element that indicates direction. In our physical world, we cannot see things with only one dimension. In art, line may be two-dimensional (a pencil line on paper, for instance), three-dimensional (like a wire in a sculpture), or implied (like the edge of a shape in a painting). They are certainly not infinite. (As I tell my students, we don't have enough time!) Lines help our eye move through the artwork. Contour lines are lines that never vary in width. They are very uniform. Calligraphic lines vary in width—think about the writing we call calligraphy and how it undulates.

2. Principles

The term "principles" refers to how the artist arranges the elements in a work of art. (Technically, the idea of color schemes should probably be discussed here, but it is not usually listed as a principle.)

Balance

How visually equal various parts of the artwork appear. There are three basic kinds of balance: formal, informal, and radial.

Formal balance is the balance of like things on either side of a center line. Symmetry is the most perfect type of formal balance.

Imagine a picture or object divided down the middle by a straight line. If the elements on one side of the line are a mirror image of those on the other, then the piece is symmetrical. Butterflies are symmetrical, and so are people. Imagine a teeter-totter with two identical twins facing each other, dressed exactly alike and seated equally far from the center. That is symmetry.

If the children on the teeter-totter do not look alike, but they are the same size and are equally far apart from the center, that is formal balance. Some people use the terms "formal" and "symmetrical" interchangeably.

Informal or asymmetrical balance is the balance of unlike things on each side of a center line. Let's imagine another teeter-totter. This time, we will balance it informally by placing a mother, who weighs 100 pounds, on one end and two children—each weighing 50 pounds—on the other end. Or, if Mom comes to the park with only one child, she might scoot in quite a bit toward the center to balance better. When an artist balances an artwork this way—by using unequal shapes or colors on each side—we say the piece is informally balanced. This is a more active arrangement than symmetry.

Radial balance occurs when a picture or object is

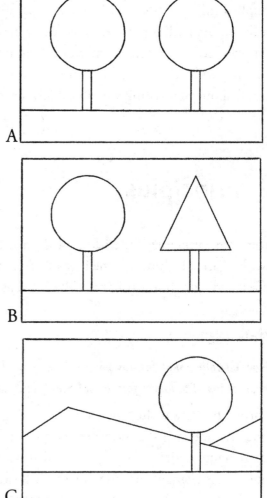

Figure A is symmetrical, figure B is formally balanced, and figure C is informally balanced.

A Brief Overview of Elements, Principles, and Other Terms

balanced around a center point rather than on either side of a center line. A merry-go-round is an example of radial balance. In order for it to run properly, the weight should be spread around evenly, not piled heavily on one side. Spirals, bicycle wheels, spiderwebs, and most hubcaps are radially balanced.

Emphasis

The principle of design by which the artist draws special attention to a particular area, object, feeling, or idea.

Emphasis may be achieved through repetition, distortion, contrast, similarity, placement, use of negative space, size, or other means. If an artist paints a bowl of apples, and all the apples are green except for one that is red, then the emphasis would be on the red apple. That is, our attention will be drawn to that one.

Contrast

The principle whereby an artist uses differences in values, colors, shapes, textures, lines, or forms to achieve emphasis, visibility, or interest.

For example, if an artist paints a pale blue circle on a green background of equal value, it might be very hard to see. The same pale blue circle on a dark orange background will attract a lot more attention! Books are printed in strongly contrasting values—black on white—to increase visibility.

Similarity or Relatedness

The use of similar but not identical elements.

This principle is used to help unify a work of art, to tie it all together. Two particular ways in which similarity is used are related shapes and related colors. Circles and ovals or squares and rectangles are examples of related shapes. Analogous colors—colors that lie next to each other on the wheel—are related to each other.

Pattern

Repetition of a motif in a predictable way.

If you can predict what will happen next in a design, it follows a pattern. A motif is the line, shape, color, form, value, texture, or combination of those elements that is being repeated. In the US flag, the two motifs are stars and stripes. The pattern is regular. If we continue the stripes from the bottom, we know that the addition will be white, red, white, red, and so on.

If I scatter a bunch of leaves onto a canvas and trace them, the pattern will be random. If I want to extend the pattern, I know the extension will involve scattered leaves, but I can't predict exactly where each leaf will be.

Unity

The sense of oneness or wholeness in a work of art.

Unity can be achieved in many ways, but the result is that when you look at the piece, nothing seems out of place or jarringly incongruous.

Repetition

The use of an identical element more than once in a work of art.

On the US flag, the stars are repeated 50 times.

Distortion

Altering an element in some way that is not its normal appearance.

The word "distortion" usually applies to shape or form. We can still recognize the subject, but it is pulled out of shape or broken up. When we walk in front of the curvy mirrors at a carnival or fair, the reflected image is a distortion of our bodies. Distortion may be used to achieve a certain style or emotional impact, as in medieval art, or to create emphasis.

Movement

How the viewer's eye is directed through a work of art.

While some works of art are very static, others may never allow the eye to rest. Artists frequently use this principle to direct our eye to the center of interest.

Rhythm

An effect that results from the repetition of an element of art.

Patterns always have a rhythm, and movement and rhythm are also closely associated.

Gradation

Going gradually from one state of an element to another.

If I go gradually from light to dark when shading a sphere, that is gradation of value. If I go from red to orange-red to red-orange to orange, that is gradation of color. If I create a row of rectangles that get gradually larger, that is gradation of size.

Simplification

Reducing a more complex shape or form to its more basic geometric foundations.

An example would be using circles or ovals for eyes.

3. Other Terms

Throughout this book, I use terms that are familiar to many art teachers. It will be helpful for you and your child to understand these terms before you begin these projects and activities.

Folds

If you have a rectangular piece of paper, there are two ways you can fold it in half. Imagine a 9-by-12-inch sheet of paper. If you fold it in half the short way—that is, if you create two 9-by-6-inch halves—we call that a hamburger fold. If you fold it in such a way as to create two 4½-by-12-inch halves, we call that a hot dog fold. If you fold a square piece of paper on the diagonal, we call that a taco fold. The side of the fold that sticks up is called the mountain, while the other side is called the valley. When you fold paper back and forth so that you alternate mountains and valleys across the page, that's called a fan fold.

Paper Orientation

You are probably aware of this concept from working on a computer. If I use a piece of paper in the portrait position, that means the longer measurement of the page is up and down. If I use it in the landscape position, the longer measurement is placed horizontally.

Types of Subject Matter

Landscape: Artworks in which the primary subjects are trees, mountains, rolling plains, or some other outdoor scene are called landscapes.

Portrait: A likeness of a particular person—especially showing his or her facial features—is called a portrait.

Still Life: Artworks in which the subjects are inanimate objects—often food, flowers, or tableware—are called still lifes.

Genre: Scenes of regular people going about their daily activities are referred to as genre pictures.

Types of Art—Approaches to Subject Matter

Following are a few of the approaches artists can take when creating a work. Please note that these approaches can overlap.

Abstraction: Abstraction is the process of analyzing, simplifying, and distilling the essence from the subject. Literally, "abstract" means to remove something, to take something out. For example, an artist looking at a landscape might abstract the triangular shapes of the pine trees or the predominant blues and greens of the scene or the textures of the leaves and grass. She might then create an artwork in which these elements are used separately from the actual scene. The original subject matter may be somewhat recognizable or completely transformed.

Realism: When the artist shows the subject as it actually appears, we call this approach realism. When an artist draws a flower that looks like the real flower, we also call this a mimetic approach.

Formalism: When an element of art is the subject of an artwork, we call it a formalist piece. For example, a painting that has green circles and blue squares used simply as shapes and colors is a formalist artwork—it is pure design. Not all formalism is totally nonobjective. For instance, cubism is a formalist approach to subject matter. Even some mimetic artists (see "Realism" above) are more focused on composition and how they arrange their shapes. Others are far more loose and expressive.

Expressionism: Expressionism can be achieved in several ways. If I paint a realistic picture of a bowl of fruit, the viewer will react to it differently than if I paint a realistic picture of a starving child. The second painting will probably elicit strong emotions. When the primary purpose of an artwork is to elicit or express emotions, we call it an expressionistic piece. One device artists use for such a purpose is distortion. Another is strong or unusual color. The way in which the medium is handled can be very expressive. If you compare the way the paint is applied to the *Mona Lisa* to the way it is used in *Starry Night* by van Gogh, you will understand why van Gogh is referred to as "the father of expressionism." When the artist does not use a recognizable subject, but rather color or texture or shape to express those emotions, we call the art abstract expressionism.

Types of Media

Following are a few of the types of media artists can use when creating a work.

Collage and Montage: A collage is a collection of *different* materials affixed to a background to create an interesting picture or design. When pieces of *one* medium (usually paper) are affixed to the background to create a picture or design, we call it a montage.

Bas-Relief, Intaglio, and Sculpture: The word "sculpture" is usually used to refer to a three-dimensional artwork that can be viewed from all sides. Michelangelo's *David* and Myron's *Discus Thrower* are both famous sculptures. Bas-relief is a form of sculpture in which the subject projects out from a background. The relief can be very deep, in which case the figures jut out and look like they are barely attached to the background. It can also be very shallow, and the figures will barely be raised off the background. (Think of a cameo or the head on a coin.) Bas-relief is viewed only from the front. Intaglio is the opposite of bas-relief. The subject is carved into a surface; it does not jut out. Sealing wax seals are carved in intaglio so that when they are pressed into the hot wax, the resulting design is a bas-relief.

Pigment: A pigment is a material that changes the color of reflected or transmitted light as the result of wavelength-selective absorption. For instance, a red pigment will absorb every wavelength of light except red. The red bounces off and hits our eye, and we perceive the object as red. (See the section on color that begins on page 3.)

Everywhere

BEFORE WE FOCUS on specific venues, I would like to suggest some general ideas that will work almost anywhere and will help accomplish some of the goals of this volume, especially helping the child to better see the world around him or her and to learn more about art.

1. Sketch Diaries

Materials
- ○ Sketch diary
- ○ Pencil

Probably the single most productive activity you can encourage the youngster to engage in is to use a sketch diary or visual journal. This can be small enough to keep in a pocket—4 by 6 inches or so—or measure anywhere up to 9 by 12 inches. I wouldn't go any bigger than that because you want the child to feel that carrying it around is easy.

I would also recommend a spiral binding or any style that allows the cover and various pages to fold completely out of the way. A simple steno pad or school notebook will work if the child can ignore the lines on the paper, but nice varieties are available at virtually any bookstore, craft shop, or art supply outlet. Some are filled with totally blank pages, and some are made with pages that are half blank and half lined.

Throughout *Art Is Every Day*, I will describe ideas for using such a journal, but you certainly don't need a specific activity. Great artists down through time have kept such diaries. They carried them and made sketches and notations of anything that caught their fancy. A regular pencil or pen is sufficient, although colored pencils can be extremely helpful. However, it is not always convenient to carry them. Very young children might carry the pad and some crayons or pencils in a small backpack. (Actually, this works for older children as well!)

A sketch diary should contain not only various drawings but notations as well. These might refer to conditions, sounds, smells, the artist's feelings at the time, a discussion of textures or colors, or thoughts for a story or poem. If the child doesn't yet read or write, you could ask her some leading questions about her drawing and jot down her answers. By giving the child the gift of such an item, you are making a statement about the importance of art and observation.

Concepts to Discuss: As noted above, you will want to stress the importance of carrying a sketchbook. Focus on the importance of noticing things in the child's environment. Also, be sure to ask to see the drawings occasionally, so that the artist understands that you truly do value his efforts. You can have some wonderful conversations about the choices the child has made.

2. Observational Drawing

Materials
○ Paper
○ Pencil

Another activity that will appear throughout this book involves observational drawings. This is exactly what it sounds like: the youngster draws what he sees. One of the most common exhortations of art teachers is "Draw what you see, not what you know." Too often we make assumptions about a subject based upon a quick glance, or we use a shorthand version for the image. An example of this is the way many children draw trees by placing a large circle on top of a stick. I would not argue that a large tree might look like this to a small child gazing up at it, nor would I deny any artist of any age the right to conceptualize or simplify an image in whatever way he or she chooses. But if you spend just a few minutes pointing out the characteristics of a real tree to a child sitting in front of it, you will be amazed at what that child will draw, and I promise you, this will in no way inhibit his future flights of imagination. In fact, you could have a great discussion about the difference between real and imaginary imagery. Perhaps after the child has observed and drawn a "real" tree, he could draw several imaginary trees as well. My guess is that the imaginary trees will be even more wonderful than before.

I absolutely believe that observational drawing is a very good addition to a child's education. It is certainly excellent training for noticing details in the world around us. There are several different approaches one can use. A quick sketch, sometimes called a gesture drawing, is fine, or the child can make a more detailed sketch, a contour drawing.

A gesture drawing is done very quickly and uses a few brief strokes to capture the essence of the subject. Perhaps you are watching a horse trot on a bridle path or a car zoom down the street. Or perhaps the subject is still, but you are moving. You wouldn't have time to draw an exact version of the experience. If you are sitting in front of a flower, on the other hand, you can include every detail. The lines used in gesture drawings, regular drawings, and sketches are often somewhat jagged.

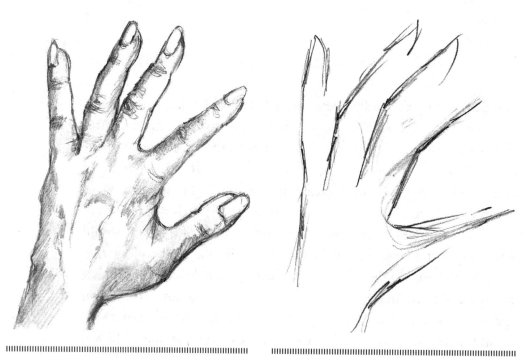

An observational drawing.

A gesture drawing.

A contour drawing, on the other hand, uses a slow, steady, contour line—a line that doesn't get wider or narrower. It can be "sighted" or "blind." In a regular contour drawing, the artist slowly follows every edge and detail of the subject, using appropriate proportions and, like the sketchy drawing, making the product look realistic. In a blind contour drawing, the artist looks only at the subject, not at the paper! He or she follows every detail, lifting the pen only rarely. The results are distorted in a delightful way. Reality, as such, is not the point, although the result is usually very recognizable. Blind contour drawing is an outstanding activity for several reasons. Among other benefits, it forces us to use a different portion of the brain than we usually do and to notice small details.

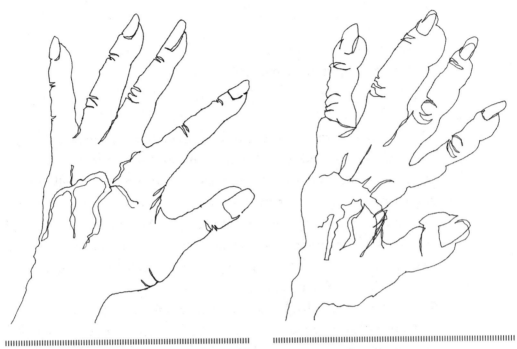

A sighted contour drawing.

A blind contour drawing.

Concepts to Discuss: Noticing details, lines, and colors is vital not only to artists but to authors, scientists, police officers, and people in many other fields. You can help your child or student develop this ability by pointing out various elements in the subject he is drawing. An added benefit of this activity is that, in order to help the artist notice added details, you will have to become more observant as well!

3. Photography

Materials
- ○ Camera (preferably digital)
- ○ Computer and printer (optional)

One of the best tools you can offer a budding artist today is a digital camera. You will find several projects in this book that will work best if you have such a device. Regular cameras can work as well, but the digital models are better in at least two important ways. First, they encourage experimentation. You are not wasting film by taking numerous shots of something. And second, you can print out the photos on plain paper on your own printer if you have one. While not totally free, these are far less expensive than commercial copies.

Good photographs display the same attention to the elements and principles of art as good paintings and other artworks. A photographer studies composition, color, shape, texture, value, line, form, balance, contrast, repetition, pattern, unity, rhythm, movement—in short, all the abstract subjects a painter studies.

A child who is truly uncomfortable drawing can learn a great deal about art by using a camera. While I strongly believe in the ideas outlined above—the sketch diary and observational drawing—these goals can be somewhat achieved using a camera. Printouts could replace drawings in a journal, and the child could make detailed photos instead of detailed drawings of a subject. In fact, students who love computers and who have access to programs such as Photoshop could turn photos into products that look like drawings. Teachers often try to grab students' attention by appealing to their interests, and an interest in cameras and computers is certainly a great beginning.

Concepts to Discuss: As you will see from the photography projects included in this book, you can use such activities to reference virtually any element of art. To focus on value or contrast, take photos in black-and-white. Essentially, you will be focusing on composition—the arrangement of the elements. Discuss such things as balance and mood. Encourage the artist to use unusual angles.

4. Rubbings

The idea of rubbing textured surfaces to transfer the texture onto a piece of paper—frottage—has been around for ages. Any child who can hold a crayon can achieve some kind of result, although you might want to help younger tots a bit. There are several instances of this technique in the book, but, of course, this is another of those activities that can be done almost anywhere.

What a nice addition to a sketch in your visual diary or to an observational drawing or photo! Here is a drawing of the bench in the park, and next to it is a rubbing of the old wood grain. Here is a terrific study of the patio furniture in the sunlight, and on the next page is a rubbing of the iron mesh.

Rubbings can transfer not only texture but writing and engraving as well. Do you have a historic cemetery in your area? How differently you will see the gravestones if you are looking for beautiful imagery to rub! You really don't need bulky materials for this. White tissue paper, the kind you place in gift boxes, will work fine if you are very careful. Unwrap a black crayon, and you're in business! (If by any chance you have the larger-sized crayon that younger children use, that's even better.) Place the tissue over the desired image and secure it in some way. (You could simply hold it for the child.) It's important that it does not move while the artist works. Then he or she uses the side of the crayon to firmly but gently rub over the paper until the desired image is transferred. This same technique can be used on the beautiful Art Deco details on a building downtown or the engraved wooden front of your antique dresser.

One of the reasons that you might want to use large sheets of tissue paper is that if the child centers it over the desired texture or image, he or she is less likely to go off the edge and get crayon on the surface being rubbed. If you are doing this activity with very small children, be sure to monitor them carefully.

Concepts to Discuss: Rubbings present great opportunities to discuss value and texture. Line can be a major factor as well, depending on the subject you choose. See the section on elements and principles for definitions of these terms.

5. Found Objects

In a couple of the projects included in this book, you will be using what artists call "found objects." These might be colorful pages from advertisements you receive in the mail, discarded boxes and bags, or organic material found in nature. Looking at things around you as potential art supplies can cause you to see them in a whole new way. You might consider filling a large box or setting aside a small area in a closet or the garage for the storage of such promising materials. While you don't want to get so carried away that you become the focus of one of those reality shows about people buried in debris, having some interesting stuff around when you or the kids feel creative can help the imagination soar. Sturdy, small gift boxes; round oatmeal containers; the tubes from paper towels or toilet paper; paper bags of all sizes; used gift wrap and ribbon; cleaned food containers; small, interestingly shaped stones; some straws from an old broom—almost anything can become something wonderful in the right hands. And thinking about objects in this way will improve creativity by helping the artist avoid a condition called "functional fixedness."

A person who displays functional fixedness sees an object only in terms of the use for which it was created. Carried to extremes, I suppose the condition would prevent us from swatting a bug with a magazine. Magazines are made to be read, not to kill insects. Most of us can see that a magazine might serve as a flyswatter, a coaster, or a fan. But consider the following scenario: a room has two strings hanging from the ceiling. People are shown into the room and asked to grab both of them, but the strings are just far enough apart that no one can do this, no matter how far they stretch their arms. In the room is a desk; on the desk are paper, paper clips, rubber bands, and a stapler. The person who can get beyond functional fixedness ties the stapler to one of the strings and swings it like a pendulum until the two strings are close enough to grasp.

Sometimes creativity merely involves looking beyond the accepted, normal uses for things. One of my favorite episodes of the television show *Project Runway* involved taking the clothing designers to a grocery and challenging them to create beautiful pieces using only what they could find at that store. A similar challenge on the show *Design Star* involved asking interior designers to create a fabulous room with materials found at a pet shop or hardware store. For the creative individual, a trip to a hardware store might yield ideas for jewelry, music, wall hangings, or sculpture!

Concepts to Discuss: You might certainly discuss form, color, or texture, depending on the found objects you are using. But you might also talk about recycling, functional fixedness, or creativity. You could pick up an empty tissue box, for instance, and make a game of describing the various things one might use it for.

6. Big Questions

On the wall of my classroom is a list of "Big Questions" that my students and I have compiled and added to over the years. Big Questions are philosophical queries that do not have quick or easy answers. They are questions that usually arise during our study of art history, but they are not specifically historical in nature.

While these topics will spark a more profound discussion with older children and teens, many of these questions can be asked in such a way as to cause even younger children to think about art in a less superficial way. One or two of these questions might be worked into a museum visit or asked while the child is drawing a picture. You might make the questions into an activity. Put each one on a slip of paper and place the slips in a jar. Each time the child comes over, pull one question out and make it the topic of discussion for that visit.

Here are my questions:

- What is art?
- Is a beautiful picture necessarily art?
- Can an animal be art?
- Can something be art if it was produced with a pattern?
- Is one person's opinion about art as good as another's?
- Is art always beautiful?
- Can a forgery be art?
- Does viewing an original provide a greater aesthetic experience than viewing a reproduction?
- Can an accident produce art?
- Can an animal produce art?
- Is there a connection between political movements and art movements?
- What makes artwork "good"?
- Can an idea be art?
- Can an object be art if its maker did not intend it to be art?
- Are all artists creative?
- What makes an artist "good"?
- Are there a limited number of colors?
- Is art getting more or less creative over time?
- Should ancient tombs and burial sites be disturbed for educational purposes?
- Can a photograph be art?

- How and when does illustration become art?
- If money is the primary motive, can the result be art?
- If money is the secondary motive, and the artist's expression comes first, is the product more aesthetic?
- Who is supposed to be satisfied by the art—the buyer, the viewer, the artist, or all three?
- Is one form of art better than another?
- Is art important to history? If so, how?
- What inspires artists?
- Is art more important in some cultures than others?
- Is clothing art?
- Are computer graphics art?
- Are video games art?
- What makes art valuable?
- Is there such a thing as absolute red, yellow, blue, or green?
- Do all artists paint what they feel?
- Is there only one way to look at art?
- What is civilization?

Can you think of other questions?

At Home

THE EASIEST PLACE to work is, of course, at home, where you can gain access to a variety of materials without worrying about transporting them. And one of the easiest ways you can encourage your child and let her know that you value art is to set aside an appropriate work space and provide those materials. Some of the following projects are popular in art classes, and I have different versions of a few in my other books, but even if your child repeats them at school, he or she will simply have had some practice.

Most of these projects are suitable for several age groups. You will decide which steps can be done completely by the child and which might need some assistance. If you want more ideas, *Art Is Fundamental* has several other projects that are easily adapted to home use. Remember, if the text contains art vocabulary that is unfamiliar, check "A Brief Overview of Elements, Principles, and Other Terms" on pages 3–16.

1. Color Mixing

Materials

- ○ 3 glass or ceramic bowls or used frozen-dinner containers
- ○ Water
- ○ Red, yellow, and blue food coloring (liquid or gel)*
- ○ Newspaper (optional)
- ○ Heavy-duty paper towels, preferably plain white

*Be aware that food coloring can stain some surfaces and is hard to remove from skin. Some sources recommend removing food coloring from hands with toothpaste (the whitening kind is best, but it won't work completely) and warm water or with baking soda. For cloth, they recommend using shaving cream.

This project is a fun way to introduce color mixing to small children, although older kids will enjoy it as well. (Smaller children may need help filling the bowls with water and adding the food coloring.)

Fill each of the three bowls about halfway with water. These bowls need not be very large—medium-sized (seven- or eight-inch) mixing bowls are fine, as long as they are made from a material that will not be stained by the food color. Flat-bottomed plastic containers, like the ones frozen dinners come in, will work just fine, and if you're working outside, you won't have to worry about breakage. If you use the latter, fill them almost full of water. Add a few drops of yellow food coloring to one container, red to the next, and blue to the last, lined up in this order. Each container of food coloring mixture should not be too watered down or too dense. You might want to put some newspaper under the bowls to catch drips.

Tear a few sheets of paper towels along the perforations. Take one square of towel and fold it geometrically. That is, fold it in half three or four times. You can fold it in a rectangular or triangular manner, and don't worry if the folded areas are not perfectly even.

The artist is going to dip the folded towel into the bowl of yellow, then the red, then the blue. It is important not to drip water from

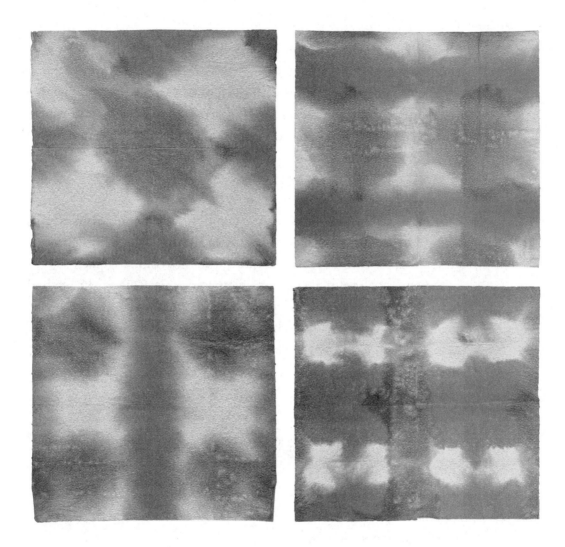

one bowl into the next, so let the towel drain a bit between dips. (You might even squeeze lightly.) The artist should place a corner or an edge in the water, not the entire wad. For instance, if the piece was folded in a triangle, the artist could dip one of the edges in the yellow, one edge in the red, and all three corners in the blue. The longer the towel sits in the water, the more color it will soak up, so you might need to add water or food coloring occasionally.

Once the artist has finished dipping, she can place the paper towel somewhere to dry. If it seems extremely wet, you might let it dry a bit before opening it, but if it seems sturdy, she can open it completely and let it dry flat. (You should put some newspaper under it to protect the countertops.)

You can do various things with the results. One possibility is to glue several pieces together to make a larger work. If the dried project is too creased to lie flat, you might try ironing it carefully. See an example on page C-2 in the color section.

Concepts to Discuss: As stated above, this lesson focuses on color mixing, specifically mixing primaries. Look closely at the results of this activity to see subtle variations. Can you find secondaries? Intermediates? What do you see where all three primaries come together?

You might also discuss pattern when doing this project. The method described should result in a regular pattern.

As you work with this technique, you will develop variations, such as making more or fewer folds as you dip or playing with other colors.

2. Photo Design Quilt

Materials

- ○ Quilt patterns
- ○ Paper
- ○ Scissors
- ○ Digital camera*
- ○ Printer*
- ○ Glue
- ○ Ruler (if copying by hand)

*If a camera and printer are not available, newspapers or magazines can be used.

In this project, the artist is going to interpret the idea of a quilt in a different medium. It is also an enjoyable way to incorporate some basic geometry into a student's day.

The first thing you will need for this activity is a variety of quilt patterns. You can get these from books at the library or download them

from the Internet. One site for free patterns is www.freepatternsonline
.com/quiltpatterns2.htm. If you can download or photocopy a block
pattern, that's great. If not, copy the chosen block onto a piece of paper.
Depending upon his or her age, you might have the child copy the
pattern anyway—it's a nice use of geometry. The block should be fairly
large, and you should make two of each design. A pattern downloaded
from the above website is approximately six inches square, which works
quite nicely. If you have some graph paper, that would make copying
much easier.

If the artist were making a normal quilt, he or she would now select
fabrics for the design. There would probably be a color scheme. I would
strongly recommend having the student also start with a color scheme.
You might pick a particular color scheme to focus on or suggest that
different block patterns have different schemes. For example, you could
pick one block and do it several times, using a monochromatic red
scheme for one, monochromatic blue for another, and monochromatic
yellow for a third. You could put the three together and discuss a triadic
color scheme. Keeping the desired colors in mind, you have several
ways to proceed.

Option 1: For Those with Digital Cameras and Computers with Color Printers

Using a digital camera, the artist or you will take pictures of patterns
around the house that work with the chosen color scheme. It might
be a good idea to look over the possibilities before selecting the color
scheme. You can use clothing, dishes, lawn furniture, upholstery fabric,
wallpaper—anything that yields an appropriate, small-scale design. Be
sure that the pattern fills the frame. You can print multiple copies of
any example, so if the artist wants to repeat a pattern, which is almost
certain, that will be no problem. You might even include a solid color
or two.

Using one of the two quilt-block copies, have the artist cut out the
various shapes that are needed and lay them on the pattern printouts.
In many cases, each shape is repeated, so he will only need to cut out

one or two of them. He traces the shapes onto the patterns, cuts them out, and glues the patterns on the corresponding shapes on the uncut quilt block. (See the color illustration on page C-2.)

Photo quilt.

The artist may then trim the paper around the block. If he is planning to use a single block as the finished project, he might even up the border—leaving perhaps ¾ inch or so all around. If he is planning to put several quilt blocks together, he could trim all excess paper away or leave a bit of white between them.

Option 2: For Those Without Cameras and Printers

Follow the same steps above for securing a quilt-block pattern. Make two copies by hand.

There are now several possibilities. Perhaps there are scraps of fabric around the house. Instead of sewing these, as the artist would on a regular quilt, he could cut and paste them onto the quilt block as with the pattern printouts described above. Or he could look through magazines for correct areas of color, then cut and glue those onto the

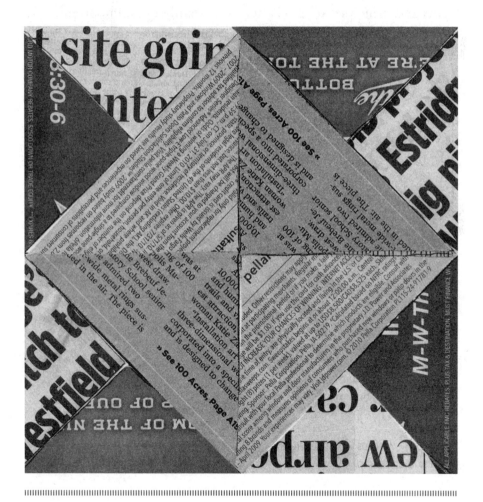

A newspaper quilt.

block. Another possibility is to use newspaper. There is a great deal of color in today's newspapers, but he could also use the printed pages as black-and-white patterns. (See the color illustration on page C-2.)

If several children are working on this project, you might have them put all of their blocks together in one artwork. If you plan to do this, or even if one child is doing multiple examples, you might suggest that there be one unifying color that appears in each block, so that the final project ties together.

Concepts to Discuss: This project encompasses many different elements and principles of art. Pattern is certainly quite important, and you might discuss regular versus random designs. You will probably use repetition, and you might want to point out how this helps tie your project together. You might notice the differences and similarities between pattern and texture. Lines and shapes will be obvious, and geometry will be present, regardless of your block choice. You could also focus a great deal on color schemes. Perhaps the child could make one block of each color scheme.

3. Paper-Bag Puppets and Masks

Option 1: Puppets

Materials
- ○ Small white- or brown-paper lunch bags
- ○ Crayons and/or markers
- ○ Colored paper and/or white paper (optional)
- ○ Scissors (optional)
- ○ Stapler (optional)
- ○ Glue or tape (optional)

Show the child a flattened (rectangular) lunch bag. You can buy these bags in packs or simply ask for one or two at a local store. Craft stores sell them in white, which would be the best, but the brown ones will work well, too.

Turn the bag so that when the bag is flat, the "flap" at the bottom of the bag is facing up. Slide your hand inside. Curve your fingers into the bottom flap and show how the bag can "talk" like a puppet. Once you have established where the "mouth" is, you can draw one on your bag; you can also add eyes. Do just enough to give the idea, then let the child create his or her own characters.

If you need inspiration, you can go to myriad Internet sites, but please don't use patterns or handouts for this project. Children can use extra paper to create limbs, ears, and tails, or they can draw these features on the bag. (You might want to use a stapler if adding these, but glue or tape will work fine as well.) The important point to stress is that the puppet is a form, and therefore all four sides must be considered. The artist cannot just draw on the front and call it a day. Unlike a two-dimensional artwork, like a painting or a drawing, a sculpture, or three-dimensional work, can be viewed from all sides, so one must make every side special. If they see a dog, a cat, or a friend from the sides or back, that view isn't blank.

This project offers many possibilities for integration. The characters could illustrate a book you have read together or a story written by the child herself. Or it could inspire the child to write a story. He or she could create a zoo or a jungle population or aliens from another planet. The puppet could be a self-portrait. This project allows even the oldest students a chance to express themselves in a fun and creative way. Fandango, a company that allows people to buy movie tickets in advance, uses paper-bag puppets in their advertisements, so many children will be familiar with the concept.

Option 2: Masks

Materials
- ○ Brown-paper shopping bags
- ○ Crayons and/or markers
- ○ Stapler, glue, or tape
- ○ Construction paper (optional)

In this age of ubiquitous advertising, most brown-paper shopping bags are covered with promotional material. If you can find a blank one, great! If you can't, you will need to work a little magic by turning one inside out. First, if the bag has handles, remove them. Then carefully pull apart all the seams. The paper overlaps, and the glue should not be so strong that you can't pull the pieces apart. But if you rip a bit, don't worry— that's OK.

Once the bag is completely opened into a single piece of flat paper, reverse all the folds—that is, take each fold and crease it in the opposite direction. All the mountains should now be valleys, and the valleys should be mountains. If you have done this correctly and you overlap the main back seam, the bag should be fairly easy to reconstruct. Then glue or tape the seams so that you have a "blank" shopping bag.

Depending upon how you plan to finish the mask, you might want to tack the bag temporarily with a little tape so that it can be flattened again for drawing.

Slip the bag over the child's head. Depending on his or her size, you might want to cut out shoulder slots on the short sides of the bag so that it fits well. (See diagram.)

Locate the child's eyes and gently make pencil marks in the appropriate spots. Of course, older students can do this step themselves. Then take the bag off, draw the eyeholes, cut them out, and decorate the bag as desired. As with the puppets described above, the point is to treat the mask as a form, not a two-dimensional shape. All four sides (actually five, if you count the top) should be considered. 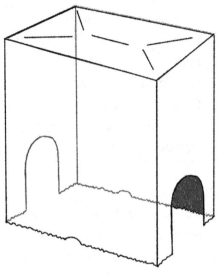 Use crayons or markers or add paper embellishments.

Once again, the opportunities for integration are infinite. Perhaps you just visited the African exhibit at your local museum or have read a book of African folk tales. African masks are wonderfully graphic and could be interpreted beautifully in this medium. Any of the suggestions mentioned above for the puppets will work here as well.

Concepts to Discuss: Form is a three-dimensional, closed figure. You might talk about how doing a puppet or mask like this is different from drawing a picture. The artist must consider the object from all sides. What other forms do you see around you?

4. Paper-Plate Masks

Materials
- ○ Paper plates (avoid using Styrofoam or plastic plates)
- ○ Crayons and/or markers
- ○ Pencils
- ○ Scissors
- ○ Tape or glue (optional)
- ○ String, rubber bands, craft stick, or unsharpened pencil
- ○ Construction paper, yarn, gift-wrapping ribbon, or fabric scraps (optional)

This project is similar to the paper-bag-mask project, but it is far more two-dimensional. Although it can stand alone, I would strongly recommend relating it to another activity, such as visiting a museum or reading a story. If a child is very involved with a specific character, such as someone from the Harry Potter series, you could create an image based on that character. Or you might look at African or Eskimo masks, Chinese *tao-tieh* figures, animals, or other images of faces that are roughly symmetrical.

Most paper plates are round, although Chinet makes an oval platter that would be fun to work with. You will probably use the underside of the plate as the front of the mask; however I can imagine situations in which you might want to use the concave side as the front instead.

This project is very simple—the child draws a face of some sort on the plate, colors it, and cuts out the eyes, adding whatever embellishments he or she wishes. The mask can be made wearable by punching a hole in each side and tying a piece of string through each hole or by cutting a rubber band and knotting each end through the holes. Another option is to tape a craft stick or a pencil to the bottom side of the plate and hold it in front of the face.

This project provides a wonderful opportunity to discuss symmetry. Most faces are generally symmetrical, although not perfectly so. You might create a very symmetrical mask, then make one that is highly asymmetrical.

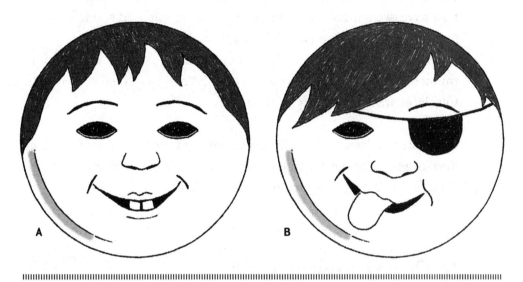

Figure A is symmetrical, but figure B is not.

You might also use this project as an opportunity to discuss realism versus abstraction. If you can view African or Eskimo masks at a museum, that would be a great introduction to such a discussion. If not, check out a book from the library that has large, colorful illustrations of African or Eskimo art. You can usually find abstractions of eyes, noses, and mouths, which are frequently simplified and sometimes highly distorted. Cartoonists often use simplification and distortion to create their characters, so this is another avenue you might explore. You might glue a large photo printout of the youngster on the paper plate and let him create a character from it. He or she might add an eye patch and a pirate's bandanna or Spock ears and winged eyebrows.

If you have access to a camera, a computer, and a photo-editing program, you can do a fun activity based on the concept of symmetry. Take a photo of the child's face or have her take one of yours. The subject should face as squarely to the camera as possible—don't look up or down or to either side. Load the photo onto the computer, and, using the photo-editing program, cut the face right down the middle and delete one half. (Be sure to save a copy of the original.) Make a copy of the remaining half, flip it, and place the two halves back together. You now have two left halves or two right halves. If you used two left halves, repeat the process with two right halves and vice versa.

Compare the results. The face in one of the new photos is probably thinner than the other, and you will usually see other differences as well. Our faces are not perfectly symmetrical.

Concepts to Discuss: As stated above, you can use this project to introduce or reinforce the concept of symmetry and/or asymmetry, abstraction, simplification, distortion, or cartooning.

5. Printmaking with Styrofoam Plates

The following activity is designed to be used at home with minimal equipment. If you are interested in a more professional or classroom approach to this project, please see pages 176–79 in *Art Is Fundamental*.

Materials
- Styrofoam material
- Ruler (optional)
- Pencil
- Scissors
- Markers
- Paper

You probably have the Styrofoam material required for this project around the house. You can use the trays that come with packages of meats, fruits, and veggies or the containers that restaurants give you with leftovers. Even certain "paper" plates are made from this foam material. While it sometimes comes in black or colors, you will want white for this activity, if possible.

Wash and dry the surface thoroughly, being careful not to scrape or dent it. You can cut out any shape, although a rectangle or square is probably easiest. Be sure to eliminate any edges that might turn up—the surface should be quite flat—but retain as much area as possible. If you are cutting straight borders, place a ruler on the surface, pull a pencil along its edge, then trim on that groove. You can stockpile such printing plates or simply let the artist prepare his or her own when you are ready for the activity.

The nice thing about this printing surface is that the child can engrave an image on it using only a sharp pencil. For a crisp, smooth line, the artist should hold the pencil at an angle and pull it in the direction of the eraser. She should not push the pencil. Surprisingly, the Styrofoam has a grain, and the pencil will move in some directions more easily than others. The line should be incised about halfway through the Styrofoam. If the child presses too hard, the line will go all the way through the plate and possibly break it. If her lines are too shallow, they might not show when she prints. Be careful with the plate—don't

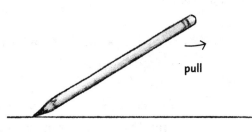

pull

dent it with knuckles or put lines so close together that a whole area is depressed. The image should be interesting—abstract designs work well, so the artist can be very free. Think in terms of lines and outlines—don't fill in shapes. And remember: the picture will print backward.

Once the image is incised, the artist may color it using markers. She can cover the entire surface with one color or use several, as on page C-3 of the color section.

The artist should try to stay out of the incised lines. I believe washable markers will work better than regular ones. Don't use indelible pens.

A print from Styrofoam plate.

The printing plate with lines emphasized.

Once the plate is covered with marker, the child may place a piece of paper over it and rub carefully with the palm of her hand. (Try to center the plate, leaving a border of white around the edge.) Because the marker or paint could be a bit dry by now, the print may be somewhat faint. For a stronger image, the artist can dampen the paper slightly and repeat the process. But it is important that the paper not be too wet. She can take a damp washcloth and draw it across a piece of computer paper. When she is satisfied with her print, it will be easy to gently wipe the plate clean and print it in other colors.

Actually, this printing surface can be used in a variety of ways. The artist can try to emphasize the incised lines as well as the background.

The artist can also use markers to draw on the printing plate without making any indentations. Once the picture is finished, she can place a piece of damp paper over the top and rub. She might even stroke a slightly damp cloth over the back of the paper while printing to "pull" the image further up into the paper. The residue of the picture will remain if she wants to recolor it to create a series of the same print.

Concepts to Discuss: When I do this project in class, I use it to focus on line, movement, and rhythm. While line will be somewhat obvious, lines used to make shapes—such as a picture of a house—could be very static. I encourage abstract designs that use many lines as lines: wavy, jagged, straight, and so forth.

If your child draws shapes, then of course you could discuss shapes. You can discuss the colors the child uses, imagery, or other elements or principles that occur to you. Once again, the opportunities for integration are many. The artist could illustrate a story, do a self-portrait, or do an observational drawing.

This project also creates a good opportunity to discuss printmaking in general. This is essentially an intaglio printing plate, but it is printed like a bas-relief. Etchings are intaglio. The ink is usually pushed down into the lines and erased from the surface, so only the lines print. A woodcut is a bas-relief. The ink is applied to the surface and the cut-away parts don't print. Depending on your circumstances and knowledge of printmaking, you might want to elaborate on these concepts.

6. Value Collage

Materials
- ○ Background surface (black, gray, or white paper or cardboard)
- ○ Assortment of colorless materials: aluminum foil, paper doilies, electrical tape, or newspaper or magazine pages (black-and-white only)
- ○ String, straws, duct tape, sewing scraps, or tissues
- ○ Glue stick
- ○ Scissors

This is a very free activity. The more materials you can provide, the more fun the artist will have. In my class, I offer the students a choice of backgrounds for this project. They may use black, dark gray, light gray, or white construction paper. If you have paper or cardboard in some value other than white, that's great, but white is fine as well. In fact, a piece of computer paper, while a bit thin, will be perfectly adequate. If the child applies a great deal of material, you can glue or staple the paper to cardboard for added strength.

Lay out the supplies and get out of the way. The child may glue materials down or use the tape you have provided. The tape can also be a medium by itself. Virtually anything goes. The child may create a design or a picture or a combination of the two. In my curriculum, this is a first-grade project, and you would be amazed by the wonderful, sophisticated results the students produce.

Tape—whether black, white, gray, or silver—can be useful not only as a medium in itself but also as a means of applying other materials to the background. Also, a large piece of aluminum foil can make a nice nonwhite surface to work on. Either side will work, and you could glue or tape it onto your paper or a piece of cardboard.

Concepts to Discuss: This is a good opportunity to discuss contrast. If the child glues a white doily onto white paper, it won't show up as well as it would on an area of silver duct tape. Sometimes artists want a lot of contrast, and sometimes they don't. White on white can be rich and elegant and subtle, or it can be boring and hard to see. A true artist thinks about the results and makes purposeful choices. That's one of the best lessons you can teach your child.

Another topic might be general composition—how the elements are arranged on the paper. Is it balanced? Is the negative space pleasing, or does the project look unfinished?

What about discussing collage? Perhaps you could find a collage on a visit to a museum. Do you have a photomontage somewhere in the house?

And of course, you will discuss value. Are there many values or only two or three? Point out that artists can make wonderful works without color.

7. Magazine Rainbow/Color Wheel

Materials
- 8-inch salad plate
- Piece of paper, 8½ by 11 inches or larger
- A ruler, protractor, or straightedge (optional)
- Markers or crayons (optional)
- Magazines, advertising mailers, or newspapers
- Scissors
- Glue stick (this will be less messy than liquid glue)

This is a terrific project on many levels. It will cause you to look at colors in a far more analytical way than ever before. You can do this activity in one sitting, or you can pull it out whenever the mood strikes. I have done it with classrooms of children, but one student can easily do it alone.

As you can see from the finished wheel shown in the color section (page C-3), I used the diagram of a simple color wheel as my starting point.

When I taught at a Jewish day school, I used a very large outline of a rainbow as the base and added Noah's ark to the result. The possibilities are pretty endless. Any image that follows the order of a prism—red to orange to yellow to green to blue to violet—will work fine. My example shows a 12-color wheel, but you might limit yours to six colors, using only the primaries and secondaries, or enlarge it to 18 by including more intermediates.

I started by tracing an eight-inch salad plate onto a piece of computer paper, although any paper will work. Using a ruler, I roughly divided my circle into 12 relatively equal wedges. (You could, however, inject one of those sly geometry lessons here, especially if you have a protractor.) You might create the outline yourself or have the child do his or her own.

||||||||||||||||||||||||||||||||||||

A magazine-collage color wheel.

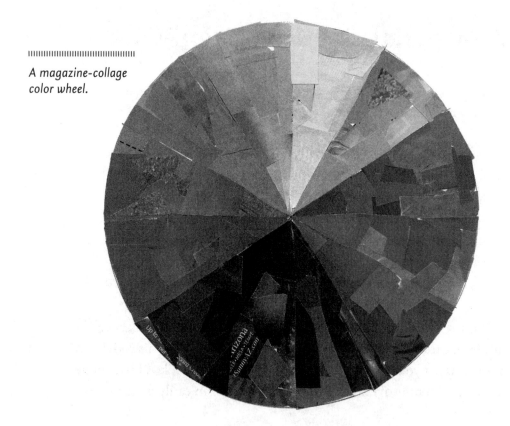

Once the design is complete, you might want to mark each shape with the appropriate color in some way. One possibility is to color in a small part of each section with a crayon or marker in your desired hue. Depending on your assortment of crayons and markers, you could at least do this in the primary and secondary areas.

If you don't have coloring materials, go through your collection of magazines, newspapers, or flyers, and pick the most perfect, truest red you can find. Cut out a bit of it and glue it in the section you have designated for that color. Repeat this step for each of the other colors. (Once again, only you know the youngsters. Older children can do this project completely by themselves, whereas you might want to give a younger child these color clues.)

The rest of the project sounds very simple—you cut out bits of color to fill each of your shapes. Easy, huh?

Not so fast! You will be amazed at how that bit of orange that seemed so pure when you saw it on the flyer looks too yellowish or reddish when placed next to the other pieces in the orange section. Actually, having more spaces—an 18-color wheel, for example—might make your life easier. In my example, you will notice a fairly sharp delineation between the sections, but when I did the rainbow, I encouraged the children to blend the edges with intermediates so that they flowed together seamlessly. The trick of this project is to spread the various colors appropriately.

You will need several copies of colored materials, so you might stockpile your magazines and mailers for a while before starting this project. (What a great way to recycle!) I will warn you in advance that some colors are much harder to find than others, but that's part of the challenge. Feel free to overlap endlessly, covering early choices with better matches as you go along.

Concepts to Discuss: This is an exercise in color theory and vocabulary. It is wonderful for introducing and reinforcing the terms "primary," "secondary," and "intermediate." However, it does far more than merely illustrate those concepts. It will help you see color in a totally different way.

8. Paper Houses

Materials

○ 12-by-18-inch white paper
(though 8½-by-11-inch computer
paper will work, too)

○ Scissors

○ Crayons or markers

○ Stapler, glue, or tape

○ Construction paper (optional)

Sculptors and architects are among the artists who deal with form, and one important aspect of their work is that they must make every side of their product interesting. The viewer should want to see all the sides, and they should all be satisfying. This project reinforces the concept that artists need to consider all sides of a form. You should probably try this activity yourself before you demonstrate it, although you may simply want to work through it together with your child.

You may use a square or a rectangular piece of paper, but a square works better, and it affords another opportunity to incorporate some geometry. You probably remember how to create a square from a rect-

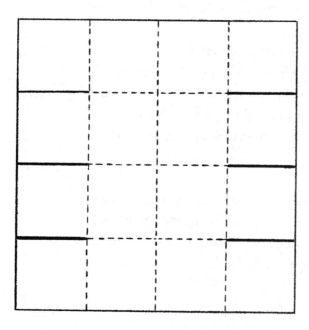

angle by pulling the shorter side of the rectangle down along the longer side until the fold hits the exact corner. At this point, you have a folded right triangle with a single flap of paper extending from it. Simply cut or tear the flap off and open the triangle to reveal a square. Fold the paper in half like a book. Open the page, and fold one of the parallel edges to the center fold. Then fold the other edge to the center fold as well. Open the paper, and fold it in half in the opposite direction (perpendicular to the original fold). Fold each of these edges to the middle. You should have 16 squares (or rectangles, if you didn't square the page). All of the mountains of the folds should be on the same side of the paper, and all the valleys on the other.

Cut slits according to the diagram.

This will result in four flaps on two opposing sides. Bring the two center flaps on one end together and rotate them toward each other until they completely overlap. This forms the roof of the house. Rotate the remaining two flaps on that end toward each other until they form the walls of the house. They should overlap somewhat and remain outside the roof flaps. Repeat this on the other edge. Do not secure the form in any way at this point. You are just seeing how the "house" will take form.

Fill in the center four squares —this will be the roof. If the artist wants to draw shingles, depending on the design, she will need to think about the direction of those shingles. If she colors the roof solidly, the direction will not matter.

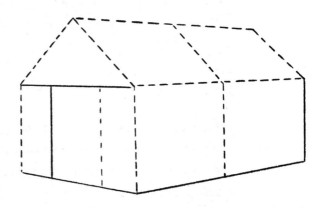

The two uncut squares in the bottom center represent the front of the house, and the two ends will wrap around to form part of the sides. The artist could cut a door or windows, and she could draw in shrubbery, flowers, and porch lights. Keep everything on this bottom strip running in the same direction. She will then turn the piece around and draw the back of the house on the two opposite center squares. It is best to

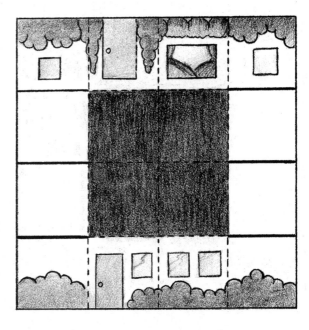

put only bushes on the end squares that wrap around, but if a child can envision where windows will end up, she can certainly include these as well. It is also a good idea to leave the two center flaps on each side, the ones that will completely overlap, totally blank.

When coloring, the artist can use markers or crayons. Once that step is complete, you may glue, tape, or staple the house so that it retains its form. The rectangle left over from creating the square can be used to make a garage, a chimney, or a dog house.

This activity can be adapted in a number of ways. The child could use construction paper and add shutters and shingles. Perhaps she could make a model of her home, then create a neighborhood complete with cars or trains. What about a farm with some cut-out animals? A downtown with different stores? If she wants to try something besides the "house" form, she could create cylinders and cones and construct a castle. What about using shoeboxes, aluminum-foil and toilet-paper tubes, and milk cartons? The possibilities are endless.

Concepts to Discuss: As stated above, the topic here is form. As in any of these projects, however, myriad other subjects might arise, depending on the kind of building that is created. Be sure that, whatever the result, it is interesting from all sides. Don't let the child deal with the front and call it a day!

9. Staring at Colors—Complements

Materials
○ Colored shapes
○ A white wall or other surface

The best material to use for the colored shapes mentioned in the materials list is the colored, clear plastic that is used for report covers. You can buy a package of these at most drugstores for three or four dollars, but the colors may not always be correct. You want a yellow, a warm blue, and a magenta (or cool red). They should match the circles in the color section (page C-4). If this is a problem, just use these circles themselves.

If you are working with younger children, introduce the subject of opposites. Ask your child the opposite of several common words. Finish the list with "black" or "white," then ask for the opposite of red. Children will make a variety of guesses. If they have not been introduced to complementary colors, they will not know the answer. Explain that just as black and white are opposites, each color has an opposite of its own, and that opposites behave in very special ways.

Explain a little about afterimages, how the brain takes little pictures of things we stare at and holds them for a very brief time. Ask your child if he has ever "seen" the bright TV screen for a few seconds after he has turned it off. Or perhaps his eye has retained the image of a lightbulb after it is no longer lit. These are afterimages. It is our ability to retain afterimages that allows us to watch movies and cartoons. If our brain did not retain a brief visual memory of each movie frame as the film went by, we would see a pretty jerky show!

Just like a real camera, our brains retain these pictures as negatives—that is, the lights are dark, the darks are light, and each color is retained as its opposite. If your children have never seen photographic negatives, it might be nice to have some handy.

Explain that our eyes have receptor cells called rods and cones. Rods receive sensations of light and dark, and cones receive sensations of color. We can "overwork" these cells. Have you ever come into a normally lit building from extremely bright sunlight? Or entered a darkened movie theater from a well-lit lobby? It can take your rods a few seconds to adjust. We can use these facts—that the brain holds a brief impression of an image, and the impression is a negative, or opposite, of the original—to find the opposite of any color we want.

Using a wall or other large white background, hold one of the acetate or paper shapes firmly against it. I usually start with magenta. Ask the child to stare at the shape for about 30 seconds. He may blink occasionally, but it is important for him to keep his eyes focused on the center of the shape.

Explain that when the 30 seconds are up, you are going to pull the shape away and that he must keep his eyes focused on the white background until the afterimage forms. This may take a couple of seconds, but you will know when he sees it, because his face will light up. Ask him what color he sees. If you held up a magenta (a cool or pinkish red) shape, the afterimage should appear to be green.

If a child doesn't see anything, it is probably because he let his eyes wander at some point. But it also could imply a color-perception problem. If this seems like a possibility, you might want to go to the library and obtain a book with color-blindness tests.

Ask the child to tell you the opposite of red. He will now say "green." Ask him the opposite of green. Most children, even young ones, will realize that it works both ways, but it is a good idea to reinforce the concept with a demonstration. (Besides, kids can't get enough of this exercise.)

Hold up all three shapes. By the time we reach this project, my students are already familiar with the primary colors red, yellow, and blue, and they know the nature of primary colors as well as how they mix to form secondaries. (You might want to wait until you have done the projects that introduce those concepts before beginning this one.)

Hold the magenta in one hand and the other two primaries in the other. Explain that even though you don't have a green shape to stare at, you do have a blue and a yellow. Place one over the other to make a green shape. It is important that all your shapes be identical so that there is no edge of another color showing. If you are using the shapes in the book, just hold up the green one, but remind the child that yellow and blue make green.

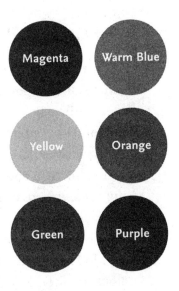

Repeat the process you used for staring at the magenta shape. When you pull the green shape away, the child should see a magenta afterimage. You can then do the same exercise using the blue acetate, which should result in an orange afterimage. Since you have no orange acetate, you will once again have to make it by mixing the other two primaries. Finally, hold up the yellow shape and stare. The violet afterimage is my favorite, which is why I save it for last. Make purple by overlapping the magenta and the blue and prove the converse by staring. By now, many of my students will be able to predict that the opposite of yellow will be purple, either because it is the only secondary left or because they have reasoned out that the opposite of each primary color is the secondary color you get when you mix the other two primaries.

Flip to the color wheel and point out that opposite colors lie directly across from—or opposite—each other on the color wheel. Explain that every color has an opposite, and that if it is a color-wheel color—not brown or ochre or a tertiary—it will lie directly across from its opposite on the wheel. Artists call opposite colors "complementary." I like to point out the difference between a "complement" and a "compliment," then discuss the root of the word "complete." Any two complementary colors actually contain all three primaries in some proportion, so in a sense you have a "complete" color wheel. You should also remind your child that because pigment and light have different primaries, the complements will be different as well.

Concepts to Discuss: The concepts involved in this particular project are explained in detail above. For more information on complementary colors, see page 6.

Red Grass and Orange Sky

Once your child is familiar with the three basic pairs of opposites, you can do an enjoyable hands-on project to reinforce the concept. You will need white paper (8½ by 11 inches is fine), pencils, and markers. If you do not have markers, use crayon very solidly and brightly.

Choose subjects that have a specific color. That is, if I say "sky," the first color that pops into your head is probably blue. As I explain to my students, artists can make the sky any color they want, and we all know that the real sky is not always blue, but for this project only we are going to use the most common color we can think of for the subject. In first grade, I use the following images: sky (blue), sun (yellow), cloud (white), brick house (red), grass (green), mountains (purple), roof (black), and an orange tree (green crown, orange oranges, brown trunk). I have also used fruits for my images, but I have found that this house-tree-mountain combination works best.

You could adapt this project in several ways for older children. You could certainly allow them to select their own subjects, provided they have a strong color association. What about flags of different countries or sports logos? It would also be a fun project to do on a computer! Have the child fold the piece paper in half, hamburger-style, to create two 5½-by-8½-inch areas. Open the piece and place it valley side up. On one side of the fold only, have the child draw the picture I just described or another appropriate one lightly in pencil. Leave the other half blank. Try to make sure the elements of the picture—the tree, the house, the cloud—are not too tiny. He may embellish the house with a door and a window. The oranges on the tree are just circles. Everything should be kept simple, and the child should try not to cross the fold line.

Now for the fun part! The artist is going to color each part of the picture in the opposite color of the one she would normally use. Ask what color one usually thinks of when someone says "sky." Most people will say "blue." Ask the child to name the opposite of blue. When he responds with the correct color—orange—tell him to color the sky with orange marker. Proceed to the next item. When you get to the tree trunk, explain that every different brown has its own opposite but that he is going to treat this brown as a dark orange. Ask him the opposite of "dark" and "orange." If you have pastel markers, you can use light blue for the trunk. If not, use a warm-blue crayon (like robin's egg or azure) or a green-blue crayon, and color lightly.

Remind the child to draw his outlines lightly with pencil first. (This will allow you to make sure he is not missing anything or that items are not too small.) He will then use markers to complete his project. It is important to color as neatly and solidly as possible. Be sure he fills the entire sky with orange, not just a stripe across the top of the page. Ask him if he can guess why he is leaving one-half of his paper blank. (Older children will probably guess right away.)

After he finishes coloring the picture in its opposite colors, he is going to stare at the center of the colored half for 30 seconds and then at the white half until the afterimage forms. In the afterimage, of course, the sky will be blue, the grass green, the sun yellow, and so on.

When the youngster finishes coloring, have him hold the project at arm's length and count slowly to 30. It is important to hold the picture still, so have him rest his entire arm on the desk or table. If he does not get a clear afterimage, have him focus on a small part of the picture at a time.

If you are working with small children, you might bring home a copy of *Hello, Red Fox*, by Eric Carle (Aladdin, 2001), which is about complementary colors.

Concepts to Discuss: You will be focusing on complementary colors, which you will find discussed in detail in the previous activity and the chapter on terms.

10. Food-Colored-String Pulling

Materials

- ○ 3 glass or ceramic bowls or used frozen-dinner containers
- ○ Water
- ○ Red, yellow, and blue food coloring (gel)* or watered-down tempera paint in these hues
- ○ Newspaper (optional)
- ○ 6 feet of kite string (cotton, not nylon)
- ○ Paper towels or rags
- ○ Paper, either 8½ by 11 inches or 9 by 12 inches

*Be aware that food coloring can stain some surfaces and is hard to remove from skin. For removing it from skin, try warm water with toothpaste (the whitening kind is best but not perfect) or baking soda; for fabric, try shaving cream.

For this project, you will need cotton kite string and watered-down food coloring. Be sure to use the gel kind for best results. Set up for this project in exactly the same way described in the first project in this section, "Color Mixing," on page 30. You will have to experiment to achieve just the right thickness of the food coloring—you don't want it too watery for this project.

Drape a two-foot piece of kite string over each container, making sure that several inches of one end hangs outside the paint. Put out paper towels or rags as well.

This project involves several different art concepts. I use it in first grade to illustrate calligraphic lines and symmetry, but it also exhibits movement and rhythm and reinforces the use of primary colors.

Ask the child if he or she knows what calligraphy is. Calligraphy is the art of beautiful writing, and it frequently requires special tools, such as flat-edged brushes or pens. If you can demonstrate this kind of line with a special marker or brush, that would be great. Or bring in some examples of calligraphy on a greeting card or from the Internet.

Discuss how lively such lines are, and point out that they get wider and narrower. Draw a contour line near a calligraphic line, if possible, and show the difference. (A contour line stays the same width all along its length. See the illustrations of contour drawing in the "Everywhere" chapter, page 21.) Explain that you are going to create calligraphy-style lines in a very special way.

In this project, each artist needs a partner. If older students do this, a partner is still a good idea, but if a person does it alone, a fairly large, heavy book might come in handy. You can certainly partner your child, but if you are entertaining more than one child, they can simply partner each other. The participants take turns being the artist.

Fold a piece of 9-by-12-inch white paper in half, hamburger-style. Open the paper and place it with the valley (inside) facing up. Starting with the yellow, the artist picks the string up by the clean end and holds it over the container. Then, pinching the place where the color starts lightly between the thumb and forefinger of her other hand, she pulls up on the string, keeping her hands over the container. This strips off excess food coloring. (Don't pinch too tightly or you will remove too much pigment, and the project will not work well.) The artist can briefly wipe her two fingers on a paper towel, then lay the colored part of the string over one-half of the paper in an interesting swirl pattern, leaving the clean end hanging off the edge of the paper. She should close the paper, then have her partner press down firmly on top with both hands, fingers splayed, while she pulls the string out. The pressure should be strong enough to offer some resistance, but not so strong as to prevent the pull. It should make a noise. (An older child or adult doing this project alone can press down with a book.) She should pull straight out, not up. After placing the yellow string back in its container, she should open the paper and repeat the process with the red and then again with the blue. (This order will prevent the colors from ruining the pigments and muddying the strings.) Wonderful symmetrical patterns result from this procedure, as well as lively calligraphic-type lines that display a great deal of movement. See the example on page C-5 of the color section.

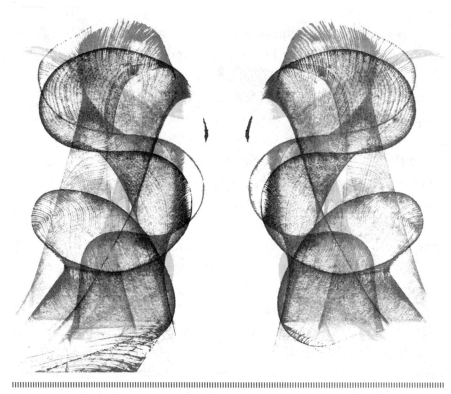

The string-pull project.

An interesting variation of this project involves using only black ink or watered-down black paint. The pulling process is the same, but once the piece is dry, the artist can enhance the design by drawing on it with a black fine-line felt-tip pen or other colors. What images do you see?

Concepts to Discuss: This project can be used to focus on a variety of concepts. Line quality, symmetry, movement, primary colors, and even imagination ("What images do you see? What does this remind you of?") are all possible topics for discussion.

11. What If You Illustrated This Story?

Materials
○ Paper
○ Pencil
○ Crayons, markers, and/or colored pencils (optional)

As you have probably realized by now, I am a firm believer in integrating subjects across the curriculum. My first book, *Art Matters*, is based on the premise that the more we integrate various subjects with each other, the better the chance that a student will learn. There is no reason that this philosophy cannot extend to projects outside school.

Real-life activities do not occur in a vacuum. Musicians use beautiful images to inspire songs, artists draw scenes from history, writers base novels on scientific facts or sociological studies, and computer programmers integrate music and art into the software they create. In a good school program, children are encouraged to see these connections whenever possible.

If you are using this book, you care a great deal about your child's education and development, so you no doubt encourage him to read. Whether you are dealing with a preschooler or a teenager, this activity is appropriate.

There are several ways to proceed. If you are working with a younger child, explain that you are going to read a new book, but you are not going to show her the pictures. Give the child paper, a pencil, and any other handy drawing materials and suggest that she illustrate the story herself. You might pause at graphic moments in the narrative or read the entire tale first. You will know the story and the artist best. If you are working with more than one child, you might suggest they work where they cannot see each other's papers, then contrast each child's vision of the tale. You can also discuss how the child drew the story in comparison to the professional illustrator.

You can encourage older children—even teenagers—to illustrate books they are reading. How would this look as a comic book or graphic novel? What scenes would you pick to illustrate? Are there certain colors you would use for mood? Students who do not like to draw could find images on a computer or in magazines or newspapers to create illustrative montages.

There are myriad possibilities for using this idea. For instance, the student need not read a story someone else has written but might write an original tale. A friend of mine who taught high school English had her students illustrate each other's descriptive paragraphs. The better the writing, the easier it was to visualize the scene and draw it.

Concepts to Discuss: What concepts do art and literature have in common? What aspects are different?

12. Still Life/Portrait/Landscape/ Genre

Materials
○ Paper or sketch diary
○ Your choice of drawing materials, such as crayons, markers, or colored pencils

One of the reasons for using this book is to help introduce your child to the vocabulary of art. When the youngster gets ready to draw, there are several types of subject matter you can suggest. One possibility is to set up a still life of interesting objects around the house. This could be as simple as a lush green plant. Or you might put some fruit in a bowl and place a pitcher next to it.

Another possibility is to have the child do your portrait, or you could arrange a drawing space in front of a mirror so that the artist can see herself and create a self-portrait. If you are working with more than one child, have them draw each other. I used to pair my students and have them draw the person across from them. Or find a face in a magazine and have the child interpret that.

The next time the weather is nice, suggest that you sit outside and draw the trees in the yard (a landscape) or the cityscape that surrounds your home. Another possible subject would be genre. Genre paintings and drawings depict normal people going about their everyday activities.

Children can make pencil sketches or use any medium they desire for these drawings. The works can be realistic or abstract, colored or black-and-white. The idea is to introduce some of the various types of subject matter that youngsters might find in a museum.

Concepts to Discuss: This is a great time to have a discussion about what artists choose as subject matter and why. Did your child enjoy drawing the face more than the plant? Is one approach more difficult? More colorful? Do different subjects give you a different feeling? Artists think about these questions as well. Do all artists choose recognizable subjects?

13. Drawing with Black Crayon

Materials
- ○ Black crayons (or charcoal)
- ○ White paper
- ○ Colored paper (optional)
- ○ White chalk (optional)

As you read on page 6, value refers to how an artist uses light and dark. In most artworks, the lightest light is white and the darkest dark is black. Middle values can be colors, but artists can create wonderful pieces without using color. Think of landscapes from China or Japan that imply many colors but use only black ink diluted to create various values. Perhaps you have an etching or lithograph around the house that can demonstrate how effective value can be without color. The following project is quite easy, but it can result in some very sophisticated work.

Give the child white paper (the lightest light) and a black crayon (the darkest dark). The youngster may turn his paper either way and draw any kind of picture or design, but encourage him to create as many values as possible.

Remind him that white is a value, so parts of the page can certainly be left blank. Ask him to create gradation somewhere on the page. Gradation will involve changing gradually from light to dark or vice versa. (For older children, you might use charcoal or Conté crayon.) When extremely different values are placed side by side, they create contrast. The closer the values, the less contrast and the harder the difference is to see. Strong contrast of value creates more visibility. Books are usually written on white or very light paper with black ink. If they were written with medium gray ink on a light gray background, we would get eyestrain pretty quickly!

There is one other concept you might use effectively in this project. Observational drawing is an extremely important aspect of a child's art experience. You might put objects on a table and have the youngster

A first grader created this lively image.

render them instead of just drawing from his imagination. I have used plants and ship models and even other pupils, or you could allow the child to explore the room to find a subject that interests him.

Another possibility is to do the project using black crayon and white chalk on colored paper. (White crayon does not cover most colored papers all that well.) This combination produces tints (colors with white added) and shades (colors with black added), although you may have to stand back a bit to see them.

Concepts to Discuss: This project is predominantly about value, but gradation and contrast should be factors as well. Artists need to know how to manipulate their media to create gradation in order to shade curved surfaces, and contrast is necessary for visibility.

14. Paper Weaving with Magazine Pictures or Newspaper

Materials

- Pictures from magazines, as large as possible
- Newspaper
- Scissors
- Glue stick (optional)
- Colored paper (optional)
- Digital camera and printer (optional)

Option 1: Focusing on Pattern

If you are really getting into the vocabulary aspect of these projects, you might want to start this activity by discussing the difference between elements and principles. The elements are the building blocks of an artwork—the colors, values, shapes, textures, lines, and forms that combine to make what we see. A principle of art refers to how an artist uses the elements. You might ask your child, "If I handed you and several of your friends a piece of black construction paper, some white string, four red circles, five blue squares, three yellow triangles, and a piece of rough fabric each, and I told you to use them in a work of art, would all of your projects look alike? Of course not! Some of you might overlap your pieces. Some might use all the circles, creating repetition, while others might choose to use only one. Some might arrange their elements symmetrically, while others would scatter theirs. Things like balance and overlap and repetition are principles of art."

One principle of art that can be illustrated by this project is pattern, and pattern requires repetition, another principle. A pattern occurs when there is enough repetition to predict what comes next. Depending upon the age of your child, you might discuss the meaning of "prediction." It's basically an educated guess about the future. If you say, "One, zero, one, zero, one, zero, one...," or "Circle, square, triangle, circle, square, triangle, circle, square...," and ask what comes next, the child will probably guess correctly. Because of the pattern that you have established, she will easily guess zero or a triangle. A pattern provides enough repetition to allow us to make an educated guess as to what comes next. You might discuss someone who makes predictions each day—for example, a meteorologist. You could discuss how repeated meteorological events allow meteorologists to see patterns, which in turn allows them to make guesses about the future.

There are two kinds of patterns you might discuss: regular patterns and random patterns. Regular patterns are pretty self-explanatory. The US flag, for instance, has a regular pattern of stripes and also of stars. A random pattern can be a bit harder to explain. Once again, depending upon the age of the child, you might need to discuss the meaning of the word "random." Once you have elicited the information that it means "haphazard" or "unsystematic" or "in no particular order," you can ask how we could possibly have a random pattern. (You might even discuss oxymorons here.) The concepts certainly seem contradictory. You might explain it this way: "Let's imagine an artist has a big canvas on the floor of her studio. She goes outside and gathers a huge armful of maple leaves, stands in front of the canvas, and scatters them all over it. Wherever they fall, she traces around them. The canvas is so large, however, that about three feet on one end is still empty. What must she do to finish the design?" When your child responds that she must gather more leaves and dump them over the empty part, ask, "What kind of leaves? Should she line them up?"

A random pattern does not allow us to predict specifically, but it does allow us to predict generally. Your child will know that the design will continue with maple leaves and that they will be scattered. If you look around the room you are in, you might find several patterns. Some, like stripes, might be very regular. Some, like many floral patterns, are seemingly random. With older children, you can simply discuss the nature of regular and random patterns.

Once you have established the concept of pattern, discuss how patterns and textures are similar—that what they have in common is repetition. One grain of sand does not make a sandy texture. Even two or three grains are not enough. I need many grains—lots of repetition. You might discuss the fact that if we look at a texture under a microscope, it would create a pattern. Look around the room at your furniture, wallpaper, carpet, and even the clothing you are wearing. Some fabrics are patterned but flat—the pattern is printed on the surface or woven in such a way that there is no texture change. In other cases, the pattern creates a texture, as in certain knits. Or you might say the texture creates a pattern. Different fabrics will suggest different possibilities for discussion; the pattern and texture are separate, the pattern creates the texture, the texture creates the pattern, and so forth. You might have an old sweater or an afghan on hand that would be a great example.

Once you have illustrated the point, you could talk a little about weaving. Your knowledge of the process and the age and experience of the child will determine the nature of the conversation. In this project, you are going to use a paper loom that will also serve as the warp (longitudinal) lines. Your wefts (crossways weaving) will also be made from paper.

Select a picture from a magazine. Try to find one that fills a page. The child should carefully cut the picture into horizontal strips about ½ inch to ¾ inch wide. If you feel the child is too young to make fairly regular strips, you could cut up the picture he chooses. Lay the strips in the order in which they were cut. Next, select a piece of paper for the loom. This might be construction paper, printer paper, another magazine photo, or a piece of newspaper. It should offer a nice contrast in color or value to the original picture. The size will be determined by the picture or piece of paper you have chosen for your weaving strips. The loom should be roughly the same size—at least an inch longer top to bottom and the same size or a bit narrower side to side.

The artist should fold the paper in half so that the top meets the bottom, and hold the still-folded page so that the fold is at the bottom. Coming in about an inch or so from one side, he should cut from the bottom fold up, stopping about ½ inch from the top. He

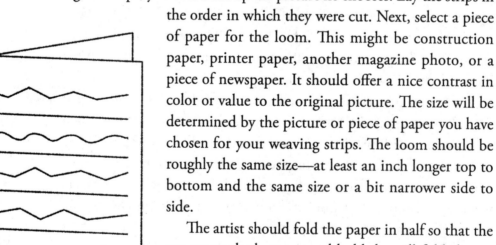

↑ **fold**

should then move his scissors over about an inch from the last cut and make a similar cut. He then repeats the process until he is within an inch or so from the other edge.

These cuts can be straight or curvy or zigzag. They can create a regular or random pattern. The important thing is that the cuts don't come too close to each other or to the edges of the paper. Keep stressing that the cuts must begin only on the folded edge. (Rather than use an inch as your measure, you could tell your child to use the distance between two knuckles on a finger.) Open the loom.

The artist is going to use an "over one, under one" basic weaving technique. Each row should be the opposite of the previous one. Make sure the weaving is tight—that is, don't leave spaces between the strips. They should touch corner to corner. Add strips until no more will fit. When the weaving is complete, the artist might dab a bit of glue on the end of each strip to keep it in place.

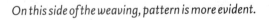

On this side of the weaving, pattern is more evident. *On this side, the bird is highly distorted.*

Paper Weaving with Magazine Pictures or Newspaper

One of the great things about this project is that both sides of the weaving are interesting. If you look at the example in the color section, you will see both the front and the back of the same weaving. One side focuses on pattern, while the other side involves distortion, which I discuss below. See page C-5 in the color section.

There are many other ways you can do this project. You could mix up the magazine strips instead of keeping them in order. Or you might not use magazine strips at all. If you have colored paper, you can use one piece for the loom and cut up one or more of the other colors for the strips.

The concept of pattern is most obvious in this approach. Did the artist choose a regular repetition—like red, blue, red, blue, red, blue— or a random pattern—like red, blue, blue, red, red, blue, red, blue,

A first grader created this super weaving.

blue, blue, red, blue, red? You might even weave a white loom with white strips and discuss texture more than pattern. You could slide toothpicks under the strips for an interesting twist on this approach.

Option 2: Focusing on Distortion

As I mentioned above, another principle you could focus on is distortion. If you used two magazine photos, what you might notice more than the pattern is how you have distorted the images. Distortion is a bit difficult to define for a younger child. In class, I use lots of illustrations. I have large glass building blocks, pictures drawn on stretchy fabric, pieces of broken mirror glued to a background, and other items. You could have your child look at her face in the bowl of a spoon or reflected in a chrome faucet. While the dictionary definition usually refers to altering the appearance of shapes, we talk about distorting sound and distorting the truth when we discuss this term. Of course, older children may have a good grasp of the concept already. I have written more about distortion in activity 17—"Distortion with Drawings, Magazine Pictures, or Printouts"—of this section (page 77).

I have already explained how distortion can be achieved by weaving magazine pictures. In fact, any weaving of a picture will distort it to some extent, but there is another way you can approach distortion that should greatly appeal to older children.

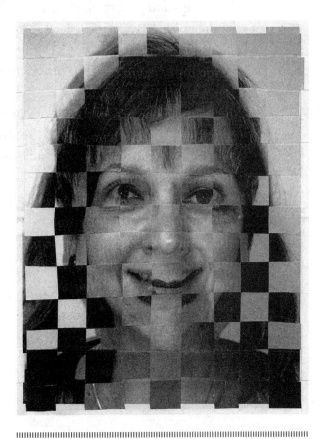

This weaving blends my assistant's face with mine.

(Younger students will love it, too.) This option requires a digital camera and a printer, although if you have two photos of faces the same size that you don't mind cutting up, those will work as well.

Take a digital picture of your child. If you are working with only one child, you could have that child or someone else take a photo of you. If you have more than one child, then photograph each one. Make sure every subject faces directly forward and that the face is unobstructed. Print these photos on regular printer paper. The only difficult part of this project is making sure that the faces are roughly the same size and location on the page. The artist selects two different faces and, using one as the loom, cuts the other into strips for weaving. This should result in a blend of the two faces—a distortion of each one.

If you don't want to weave the faces, the artist could cut both photos into strips and glue them onto another piece of paper, alternating pieces as she goes. That is, take piece 1 from photo A, piece 2 from photo B, piece 3 from photo A, piece 4 from photo B, and so on. You could make a second picture using the alternate pieces from the two photos and compare the two.

There are wonderful variations on paper weaving in books or on the Internet, or perhaps you might be able to use real looms and yarn, or grasses, or strips of recyclables such as newspaper or trash bags.

Concepts to Discuss: As outlined above, depending on your approach and its result, you might focus on such principles as regular or random pattern or distortion. Repetition will definitely be involved, and you can also incorporate the element of texture.

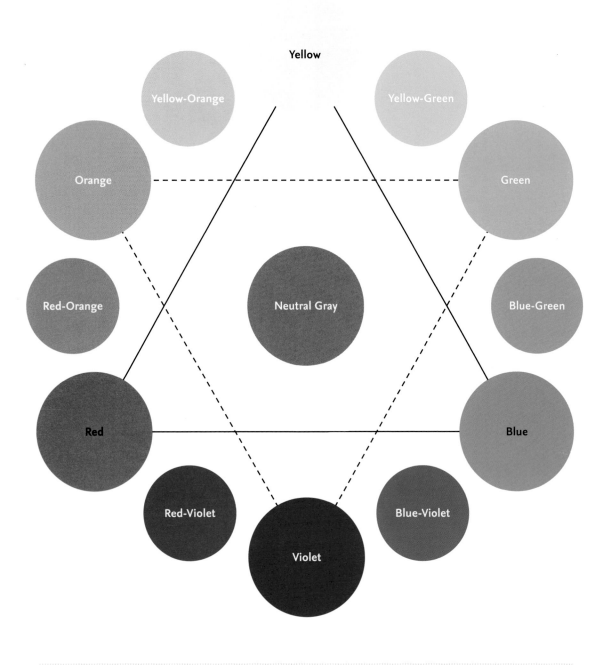

A very basic color wheel.

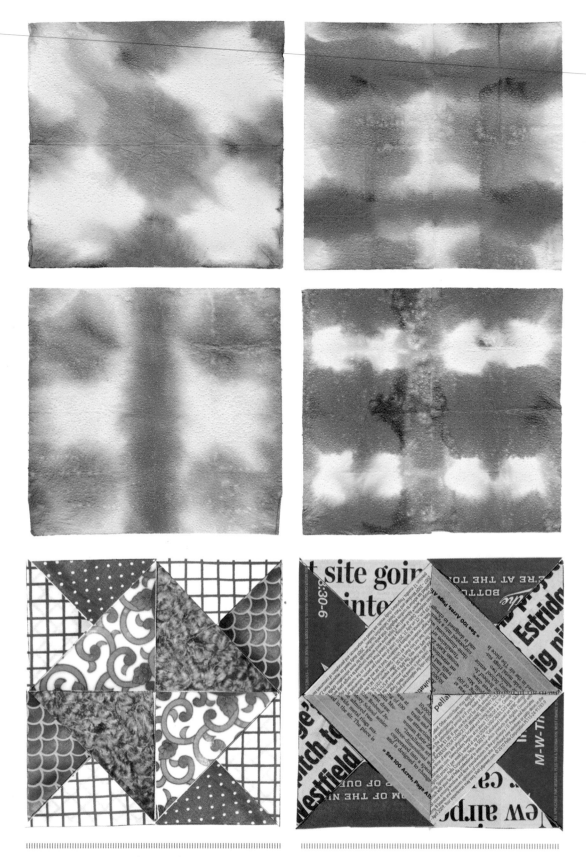

A photo quilt.

A newspaper quilt.

A print from a Styrofoam plate.

The printing plate with lines emphasized.

► A magazine-
collage
color wheel.

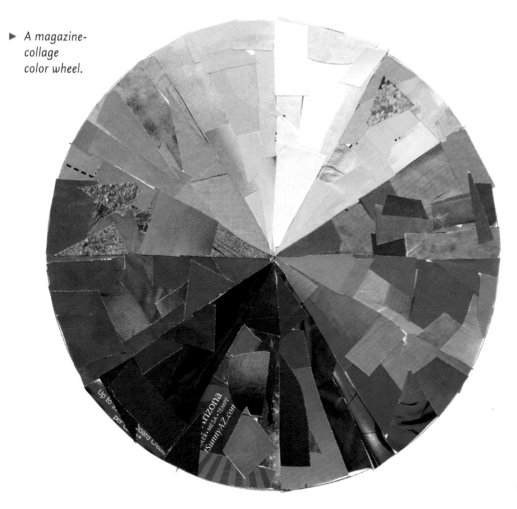

C-4

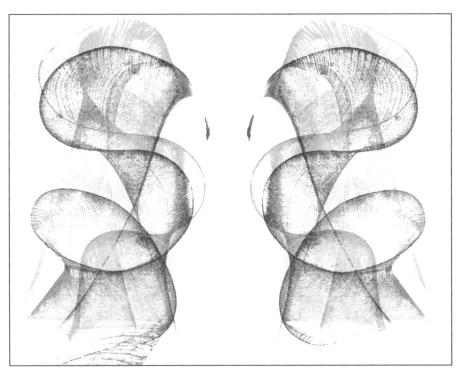

◀ *The string-pull project.*

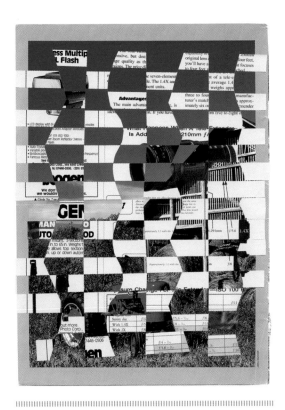

On this side of the weaving, pattern is more evident.

On this side, the bird is highly distorted.

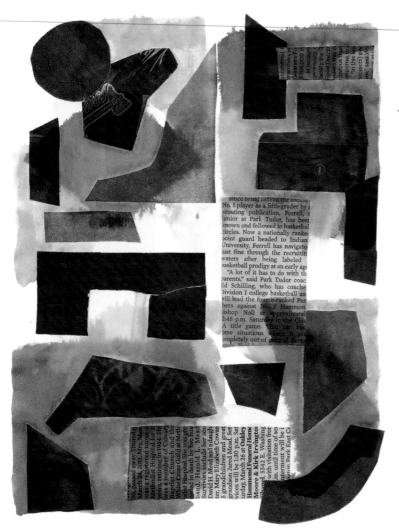

▲ *Newspaper values and food-coloring paints.*

A second grader used drawings to make this lovely distortion project.

◄ This design was produced with a carved potato.

A fall tree created from mixed colors looks far different from one drawn with one crayon.

▶ This tree was drawn using only
red, magenta, blue, sky-blue, yellow,
and lemon-yellow crayons.

15. Interpret Values with Newspaper

Materials

○ White paper (heavier, like construction paper, if possible)

○ Newspapers and/or magazines

○ Any other flat, colorless materials (silver or gray wrapping paper or black or gray construction paper—optional but recommended)

○ Scissors

○ Glue

○ Watercolors and brush

○ Water (food coloring can be used instead of watercolors)

The white paper will be the background of this project, which is all about value. Going through the newspapers or magazines, locate areas of pure value: black, white, and gray. Try to find large areas if possible, cut them out, and set them aside. Point out that areas of print can be read as gray. You might use other materials that have pure value, such as tape or wrapping paper.

There are two distinct steps to this lesson. In step one, the child glues shapes cut from the various values of materials onto the chosen background to create a picture or design. Encourage the youngster to balance the darks and lights as well as possible. For instance, if you see all the darks on one side, suggest that perhaps some dark would look great on the other side as well. Make sure that the edges of all the pieces are carefully glued—nothing should be loose.

Step two requires watercolors. Tell the child she may use anything in the paint box except the black, and she should not use the pigments too thickly. (If she is using food colorings, she shouldn't water them down too much.) If the watercolor looks opaque or sticky, suggest that she add more water. The value structure will be provided by the underlying montage. The child will simply paint a picture or design right on top of the picture or design she created with the cut and glued papers. She

Newspaper values and food-coloring paints.

should be encouraged to go off the underlying shapes. That is, an area of color should cross several values. The relatively thin washes should allow the values to show through. For example, she might put clouds of grays, newspaper, and black on a white area, then paint the entire "sky" with a thin wash of orange or blue.

The easiest approach to this project is to paint an abstract design over a different, albeit related, design. Where the wash goes over white paper, it will create a tint. Where it covers black or dark gray paper, it will yield a shade. Gray papers can also yield a less intense tone. You might need to touch up the gluing after the paint has dried.

This is a nice way to encourage children to consider the importance of value structure in an artwork. See the color example on page C-6.

Of course, like any other project, this one can be very simple or extremely complex. For instance, an older artist could print a black-and-white photo of a face, or draw one, then fill in the areas with the cut materials in appropriate values and paint it using either realistic or expressionistic colors.

Concepts to Discuss: There are several terms you can discuss during this activity. You could introduce or review the concepts of value, tint, and shade. Some of the colors will be more intense than others, so you could explore brightness and dullness. Balance is also an issue, especially when dealing with values. You could even focus on the nature of watercolors—how the addition of water makes them less intense.

16. Using Line to Create the Illusion of Form

Materials
- ○ White paper
- ○ Pencil
- ○ Marker (black or any dark color)

This activity produces a delightful illusion that kids enjoy. I do it in second grade, and it is a bit challenging for some of my students, so you might want to consider your child's age when choosing this project. The purpose of the activity is to use lines to create the illusion of form.

The artist should place a piece of white paper (either 8½ by 11 inches or 9 by 12 inches) in the portrait position, then place his nondominant hand and bare forearm on the page in such a way that it fills the paper nicely. He should splay his fingers slightly but make sure his thumb is generally vertical, not parallel to the top of the page. Then he should trace his hand and arm very lightly with a pencil.

Using a dark-value marker, the child should start at the bottom of the page and draw a straight contour line parallel to the lower edge. When he comes to a pencil line, starting right on the pencil line, he should curve the line up slightly. He will curve back down to the next pencil line, and then continue parallel to the lower edge to the end of the page. He should try to align this part of the straight line with the starting line. He will then repeat the process about ¼ inch above the first line and continue up the page, keeping all the straight, horizontal lines as parallel to each other as possible. When he comes to fingers, the theory is the same. He should curve up on the first pencil line, back down to the second, up on the third, down onto the fourth, and so on. All lines traversing negative space should be parallel to the top or bottom.

This lovely piece was done by a second grader.

Actually, the artist need not start at the top or bottom of the page. He could start in the middle and move up and down. One nice aspect of this project is that a child can fill in large gaps without going completely across the page, and it will not be particularly noticeable. Be sure the marker lines change direction sharply on the pencil lines, not somewhere in the general vicinity. Do not trace the pencil line itself with marker.

You can do this project with objects other than a hand. The object should be relatively flat and big enough to work with, such as a pair of scissors.

Concepts to Discuss: This activity is rife with vocabulary. You could discuss the nature of a line, specifically a contour line. You will certainly want to discuss the nature of form as well as the concept of an illusion. You might even include the concept of parallel lines.

17. Distortion with Drawings, Magazine Pictures, or Printouts

Materials

- Two images exactly the same size and orientation (these can be drawings, magazine photos, or computer printouts)
- Pencil
- One sheet of paper the same height and twice as wide as one image
- Scissors
- Ruler
- Glue

I have several things in my classroom that can demonstrate distortion. One involves drawing simple pictures, such as the outline of a shark or a dolphin—or any shape, actually—on pieces of stretchy white fabric using an appropriate pen. (This could be a project in and of itself.) Even if you don't create such visual aids, I'm sure you have something around the house that demonstrates distortion. Some sort of "bubble" glass? A rounded chrome surface, such as a faucet or a spoon, that reflects your face? Glass block windows or shower enclosures? You might introduce the idea by referring to the mirrors one sees at carnivals. We fortunately have these mirrors at our local children's museum, so most of my students are familiar with them. But if your child is not, you can discuss the concept using one or more of the objects mentioned above.

The key aspect of distortion is that you should understand that it is a distortion—you must know what the "real" object is. For instance, if you draw an amoeba-like shape on a piece of paper, no one knows if it is meant to be a distorted circle or an organic shape. If you draw a squiggly humanesque shape, however, children will know it is a distorted human figure before you are halfway around it. In art, as well as in the dictionary, distortion usually refers to shape or form, although we can distort virtually any element. Distortion is a little hard to put into words, but essentially it means to change something from its natural appearance in such a way that we can still tell what it originally was.

You might explain that the word does not just apply to art. We can distort the truth. If you go fishing and catch a 10-inch bass, but you tell your friends it was a two-foot whopper, you are exaggerating. Exaggeration is a form of distortion. We can also distort sound. Many children are familiar with the electronic gizmos that change the sound of guitars or voices. I discuss the fact that in the old days, records had three speeds. For fun, children would play records at the wrong speed, making them sound slow and deep or fast and high, like Alvin and the Chipmunks.

Once your child is comfortable with the concept of distortion, you can begin to explain the project. There are several ways you can do this, depending upon the materials available and the age of the artist. One option is to have the child make two drawings. You can use computer paper, but be sure to orient both of them in the portrait position. The youngster can use markers or crayons or even watercolors. The two pictures can be totally different. One might be a design and one a picture, for example. Or they can be very similar or related in some way, like a dog on one and a dog house on the other. The image should stretch completely across the paper. It need not actually touch the sides, but it should come close. There should be no tiny little shapes. The artist may leave negative space (or not), but most of the paper should be covered with the image. If you use drawings and the child is young, you will want to differentiate the papers in some way. You might color the back of one lightly with a yellow crayon, for example.

After the child has finished a page, you are going to draw lines on the back in one-inch vertical strips. (Older children can do this step themselves.) The easiest way to do this is to cut a piece of cardboard a smidge less than one inch wide and at least as long as the height of the pictures to use as a guide, but you can certainly use a ruler to mark off one-inch increments on the top and bottom and connect the dots. If you do use a ruler, make sure your top and bottom measurements start from the same side. If you used computer paper, the last strip will only be ½ inch. After the back of the page is divided, number the strips from one to nine, starting on the right-hand side. Looking at the back of the drawing, the first number on the left is nine and the last one on the right is one.

Find a piece of paper that is the same size as both drawings placed side by side. This could be a piece of newspaper or wrapping paper or

|||||||||||||||||||||||||||||||||||||

A second grader used drawings to make this lovely distortion project.

construction paper. If the child used computer paper for the drawings, you could tape two clean sheets together side by side.

Explain that the artist may start the next step with either drawing. If you have color coded the back of one, you will be able to keep the process straight. The child should carefully cut off strip number one from one of the drawings. This will be on the right side of the back, but when she turns the strip over, it will be the first strip on the left of the front. The child should line this strip up carefully along the left edge of the background paper and glue it down. Then she cuts piece number one from the other drawing and glues it carefully next to the first piece. Tell the child that it is very important not to leave gaps between the pieces and not to overlap. The more carefully and straightly she cuts, the easier this will be. The artist should continue cutting and gluing one piece at a time, alternating pictures, until the entire background piece is covered. Warn her that the last strip may not fit completely on the background. The child should put the glue on the part of the background paper that is exposed and let the strip hang over. Do not trim anything off. It is also a good idea to align the tops of the strips with the top of the background so that the image lines up correctly.

After all the strips are glued down, fanfold the project, placing the folds where the strips meet. When you look at the piece from one direction, you will see one of the original images, and when you look at it from the other direction, you will see the other image. As your eye moves across the front of the project, the images will become more and more distorted until they merge. See page C-6 in the color section.

Children may adapt this project in a number of ways. They can use two magazine or computer pictures instead of drawing their own. Of course, the computer pictures could be original as well. The only requirements are that the two images must be the same size, the strips must be uniform, and the background must be equal to the width of the two images side by side.

Concepts to Discuss: This project focuses on distortion, but other issues may certainly arise, depending on the images used.

18. Drawing to Music

Materials
- ○ Music source (CDs, radio, MP3 player)
- ○ Drawing supplies

This is an extremely easy activity. You will choose some appropriate music and have the child interpret it visually. By "appropriate," I mean music with a strong rhythm or a definite mood. If you love classical music, you might want to tell the child a bit about the piece before you begin. Or maybe you could have the child draw first and then compare the drawing to the "story" the musician was trying to tell. If you choose a children's song, the story is usually pretty obvious—think "Old Mac-Donald Had a Farm" or "Itsy-Bitsy Spider."

However, you certainly need not focus on such literal interpretations. You could stress the abstract qualities of any piece of music—especially the rhythm or movement. How might the artist express the pace of the song? What if it is very fast? What if it is very slow? What about the mood? What colors or lines or shapes express happiness? Sadness? Danger? (Think *Jaws* or Darth Vader's theme from *Star Wars*.) What about the instruments? Does a piano suggest different colors and patterns than a drum? How does a horn "look" next to a harp?

You can choose any materials for this project—anything from basic pencil and paper to paints, markers, crayons, or chalk. Materials that can produce color will offer more possibilities, but the child could fill several pages with simple ballpoint-pen drawings that compare different rhythms. Then maybe he could cut out pieces from each to make a montage, or grid them together. If you have access to any blank music manuscript paper, that would make a superb background for such sketches or paintings. The main point of such activities is to focus on the similarities between art and music. Has your child learned about texture or tone color or line or rhythm in music class?

A nice twist on this theme for older children is to have them design cover art for a piece of music. This could even be done on a computer.

Concepts to Discuss: The more you know about music, the more fun you can have with this project. But even if you know absolutely no music vocabulary, this will still be a productive activity. Simply focus on rhythm or mood, as suggested above, and let the child be creative.

19. Pattern/Texture Fill

Materials
- Paper
- Pencil
- Black marker

As well as being a fun way to pass time, this project shows the importance of the principle of contrast in a work of art. You may use a regular marker or a thin one, or any type of pen that writes black.

This project offers a good opportunity to discuss the similarities between texture and pattern. They both require repetition, which is also a principle of art. You might want to read about regular and random patterns in project 14, "Paper Weaving with Magazine Pictures or Newspaper" (page 66), before you begin.

Explain that if we looked at a texture under a magnifying glass or microscope, it would appear to be a pattern. Likewise, if we viewed a pattern from a distance, it might appear to be a texture. There is no precise way to say when something stops being a pattern and becomes a texture or vice versa. The best way to decide if something qualifies as a texture is to ask yourself if it makes you want to touch it. If you think of an area as "furry" or "bumpy" or "rough," then it is a texture. If you are more aware of the repetition, it is a pattern.

A pattern is created through the repetition of a motif. The motif can be virtually any element of art or a combination of them. If you write your name over and over, your name is the motif. (The letters can be considered lines or shapes.) In a polka-dot fabric, a single dot is the motif. On the American flag, the motif for the stripes would be one red and one white. Motifs occur in music and literature. In music, the word refers to a series of notes that are repeated, and in literature, it is a theme.

The first step of this project involves using very light pencil lines to tessellate a piece of paper. Remember, we use that term loosely to mean dividing the entire page into positive shapes, with no unbroken background. The shapes should not be too big or too small. Patterns and textures require repetition, and you can't repeat a motif enough if the area is too small. The child can create a picture or a design, as long as the shapes are large enough and fairly simple. Of course, older children can produce more complicated compositions.

The child is going to fill each shape with a pattern or a texture. The scale and the motif will determine whether we see it as a pattern or a texture. Using a black marker, he will fill one of the shapes with a repeated motif, such as a dot. He should go carefully up to the pencil lines but not beyond, and use plenty of repetition to fill the area fully. Think of the shape as a piece cut from cloth. Fill an adjacent shape with a different motif, such as a line. Stress the fact that shapes next to each other must have patterns or textures that are very different, or the shape will not show. Letters, numbers, and even punctuation marks can be motifs, but if you use such motifs next to each other, it will be very hard to see where one shape ends and the next begins.

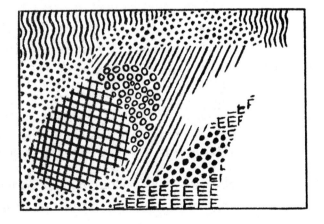

As I stated above, contrast is a very important principle in this project, and the most important kind of contrast for this project is a contrast of value. That is, when two patterns or textures lie next to each other, one should be much darker than the other. This effect can be achieved by using heavier lines or dots or by a denser use of the motif. The important thing is to fill the shape, not just put a few motifs in the center. Also, you should remind the child not to draw on the pencil lines. The only way we should know where one shape ends and another begins is by the change of pattern or texture.

Concepts to Discuss: This activity is rife with vocabulary. Motif, repetition, texture, pattern, contrast, and tessellation are just some of the concepts you might introduce as your child creates his design. See the section on definitions if you need help with these terms.

20. Vegetable Prints

Materials
- Potatoes, green peppers, or other hard vegetables
- Sharp knife
- Paper towels
- Flat containers, such as glass or foil pie plates, that won't stain
- Water
- Newspapers (optional)
- Food coloring or tempera paint*
- Paper

*Be aware that food coloring can stain some surfaces and is hard to remove from skin. Some sources recommend removing food coloring from hands with toothpaste (the whitening kind is best) and warm water or with baking soda. For cloth, they recommend using shaving cream.

If you have had a child in kindergarten or nursery school, he has probably done some version of this project. I don't think he will mind repeating it, however, and older children can create a more sophisticated result.

You will start by slicing a vegetable in half. For the simplest approach, use a veggie that makes a fancy shape when cut in half. Green peppers and onions, for instance, have designs built in if they're cut horizontally. If you are using a potato, you can carve a design into the cut, flat end. Whatever part of the flat surface you cut away will not print and the remaining flat part will. You could use a carrot for small, circular shapes. Feel free to experiment with whatever is in the fridge or pantry.

Tear off a square of paper towel and fold it in half twice to make a pad. Place the pad in the flat container and dampen it thoroughly with water. You might want to place the container on some newspapers to protect table- or countertops. Squirt or squeeze food coloring or tempera paint on the pad and use your vegetable to spread it evenly. If using tempera, don't make the pad too gloppy. Add a bit more water if necessary.

Place a clean piece of paper in a convenient place near your work area. Once your "ink pad" is prepared, the artist swirls the flat end of the vegetable around on it and then presses it firmly onto the paper. Repeat. The artist may get several prints from one application of the colorant, but he should feel free to place the veggie on the stamp pad after each print.

If the child would like to print in several colors, there are a couple of options. You could prepare several "ink pads" before you begin, or you could have the child stamp all the yellow shapes

This design was produced with a carved potato.

he desires, then throw that pad away and create a different one. If you do change colors, try to have a different piece of vegetable for each one. If that is not possible, print yellow first, then red, then blue, rinsing the vegetable as thoroughly as possible and drying it before each color change. Or you could slice a bit off the flat end each time you change colors.

This activity offers a fun way to make wrapping paper. Try using white or colored tissue paper as your background. Older children can make wonderful grid designs that echo African *adinkra* cloth or even quilts. You can get books with pictures of these designs or find them on the Internet. See the color illustration on page C-7.

Concepts to Discuss: Shape is certainly a possible topic for discussion during this activity. Did the child choose to create a geometric or an organic shape? If she is printing the natural shape of the veggie, you might talk about how different such a shape is from a square or triangle. What about color? Is there a color scheme? Did colors mix in some way to create new hues? There should certainly be repetition. Or perhaps related shapes. Pattern, whether random or regular, would certainly be a fruitful topic.

21. Homemade Play-Doh or Self-Hardening Clay

Materials (Uncooked version)

- Newspaper (optional)
- Bowl and spoon
- ½ cup salt
- 1 cup flour
- ½ cup water
- Food coloring (optional)
- Airtight container

This is an excellent activity for children of almost all ages, who will enjoy working with a malleable material like clay or Play-Doh.

It is extremely easy to make a Play-Doh-like substance at home, and the Internet has many recipes and instructions. Some of the recipes require cooking and some don't. I am including one of each kind here, but I would urge you to surf the Web for one that appeals to you. The addition of coloring of some sort, usually food coloring, is not absolutely necessary but will definitely make the activity more attractive to younger children.

The ingredients listed above will yield a malleable material without cooking. If the child is making the dough herself, you might want to spread out some newspapers on the work surface before starting, depending upon her age.

Using a large bowl, put in the salt and flour, then add the water and food coloring and stir until the mixture feels like dough. If the result is a bit sticky, add a little more flour a bit at a time until the mixture feels right.

Materials (Cooked version)

- 2 cups flour
- 1 cup salt
- 1 tablespoon cream of tartar (optional)
- 2 cups warm water
- 2 tablespoons vegetable oil
- Food coloring (optional)
- Pot
- Stirrer
- Airtight container

Some people feel that the cooked varieties of this material have a nicer texture and pliability, but younger children can make the uncooked version by themselves, while cooking will require far more supervision. For this recipe, mix all the ingredients together in a pot and stir over low heat until the mixture pulls away from the sides of the pan and clumps in the center. When this happens, remove the pan from the heat and allow it to cool. If the mixture is too sticky, you have not cooked it enough. Return it to the stove and heat it until it has the right feel.

For either version, you should store the dough in an airtight container. Please be aware that, if left to dry, the final results can be crumbly. Also, be careful to keep the material away from your pets. If a child eats a bit, it will probably not hurt him, but if any being—a child or a pet—swallows a whole ball, the high salt content could cause severe problems.

Actual Play-Doh or other nonhardening modeling clays are nontoxic and not terribly expensive, if you would prefer to buy a product, but kids might enjoy modeling with a substance they have made themselves. If you have an older child who likes to sculpt, I would recommend keeping some nonhardening clay such as Amaco Permoplast around the house.

Whether you buy or make your modeling material, this is primarily a form project. The child should be encouraged to experiment but to consider all the sides of the final product. If you make your own dough, you could certainly include a lesson on color mixing. Food coloring comes in red, yellow, blue, and green. How would you make purple Play-Doh? Orange? Gray?

If your child exhibits a love of sculpting, you might look for a local class that uses more enduring materials, or buy some self-hardening clay or one of the many commercial products that can be hardened in an oven. Crayola has a nice assortment of modeling doughs, and other companies do as well. There are also "instant" types of papier-mâché that are fun to use. A favorite of mine is Sculptamold, made by Amaco.

Concepts to Discuss: As stated above, this is essentially a form project. However, if you do make your own compound and choose to make various colors, you might want to review pages 30–32 for tips on color mixing.

22. Building People and Cartoon Characters from Magazine Photos

Materials
- ○ Magazines or newspaper inserts with pictures of people (or animals)
- ○ Scissors
- ○ Glue stick
- ○ Paper
- ○ Drawing materials (optional)

This project is all about creativity and thinking outside the box, although it will provide a great opportunity to discuss concepts such as distortion and proportion. Essentially, the child is going to assemble a character from various body parts culled from the magazines or newspaper inserts.

Start by collecting magazine or insert pages that have pictures of people. The child cuts out heads, torsos, arms, legs, hands, and feet. This activity will be a lot more fun if the body parts are very different in scale. Then the child creates a figure by gluing down a torso and adding a head and limbs from the stack. Does she want an alien with two heads? No problem! Six arms? Odd proportions? A figure with two left feet? Enormous hands? A tiny head? The possibilities are endless, and they can be very funny!

This project need not be limited to figures. The artist might cut out eyes, noses, ears, mouths, and hair to create an unusual face. Or perhaps your child wants a robotic creature with cars for feet. The whole point is to create a character that is unusual and fun. The youngster can then finish the paper by drawing a background or filling in missing parts or leave the montage as is.

If you have a computer and a graphics program of some sort, older children can do this project digitally using images from the Internet. Or you could take digital photos of each other, upload them, and use them to assemble the new character. How would your son like to see himself with a huge head and small body? How would your daughter look with enormous feet?

Of course, this activity could easily lead into some creative writing or storytelling. Perhaps one of the characters created could be the subject of a children's book!

Concepts to Discuss: As stated above, this project could inspire a story or discussion of the character, but it could also spark a discussion of distortion or proportion.

23. Imaginary Shape

Materials
○ Colored paper (optional)
○ White paper
○ Glue (if using colored paper)
○ Crayons, markers, or colored pencils

This is a quick and fun activity for younger children, although it can be challenging for older ones as well. If you have ever tried to find images in clouds, you will already be familiar with the concept. The point of the project is to challenge the child's imagination.

If you have a piece of colored paper, cut an unusual shape out of it and give it to the youngster. Try to avoid geometric shapes, although angles are fine. Explain to the child that she is to look at the shape until she has an idea of what it might be, but she is not to tell you. She can turn it in any direction or flip it over. Then she glues it down and completes the picture in such a way that you can tell what the subject is. Encourage her to look at both the positive shape and its negative aspects. Sometimes it is the chunk missing from one side of a piece that becomes the focal point: a tunnel or the head of a duck. She is welcome to draw on the colored piece. She may add spots to a "dog" or windows to a "castle."

When I do this project with first graders, it is a very free project, but I do have one rule. If the student gets a red shape, let's say, he or she can't take a red marker or crayon and fill in all the irregular edges to make a rectangle or oval or some completely different shape. The student can add "tails" or "ears" or other protrusions, but the original shape must be clearly visible. Of course, you will make your own rules, but the idea is to challenge the child's imagination, and allowing her to completely transform the shape doesn't accomplish that. If she struggles for several minutes or gets too frustrated, you can offer her an alternative shape, but make sure she really tries to find an image first. When she is done with the drawing, see if you can tell what the picture represents.

If you don't have colored paper, you can draw a shape on the page. This would be a great activity to pass time while traveling. Even if the child does not have coloring materials, she can finish the drawing with a pencil.

Concepts to Discuss: While this project is truly about imagination rather than elements or principles, it does provide a nice opportunity to distinguish between geometric and organic or irregular shapes. You might also discuss positive and negative space.

At the Art Museum

WHILE THIS CHAPTER is about various projects and exercises you can do at a museum, simply visiting such a venue should start the creative juices flowing. If you focus on the more primitive or contemporary galleries, you will almost certainly find an idea or two that will inspire a personal activity you could do at home, such as the mask or quilt projects described previously. Some museums have become very hands-on and have rooms for creating projects. Since each museum is different, I am presenting ideas that should work anywhere. Most of these suggestions use very few or no materials, but they might make your next trip to the museum more enjoyable and productive.

1. Generate a Word List

Materials
○ Paper and pencil (make sure this is OK with the museum!)

I discuss the classroom use of this exercise at length in *Art Matters*. I have used it with adults and middle schoolers, and a friend used a version of it in kindergarten. It is an outstanding way to encourage the exploration of a work of art, to notice things about a piece you might otherwise miss. You can use it with any number of people, although it is a bit more fun with a group.

Years ago in my class, I used to put up a slide of a work and ask a student to describe it to someone who could not see it. They were to do so in such a thorough way that the nonseeing person could visualize it. I deal with bright, articulate children, yet I was always amazed at how incomplete their descriptions were. With this exercise, very little is missed, and it has the added bonus of being more than merely descriptive.

When one critiques a work of art, there are several factors involved. According to Edmund Burke Feldman, judging an artwork follows certain stages. We usually see the overall product first: "This is a painting of a bowl of fruit or a sculpture of a person." We notice other things as well. The artist used blue and red. The arrangement is symmetrical. These stages are description and analysis. Then we interpret. Is the artist trying to tell me something? Make me feel something? (Saying "I see a man with a crown" is descriptive. Saying "I see a king" is interpretive.)

Finally, we are ready for judgment. Based on the first three steps, do I feel the artist was successful in what he or she was trying to achieve? If the goal was to tell me a story about a battle, did I understand it? If the artist wanted me to feel sad about the fate of a mother and child, do I feel sad? This activity can encompass all of these approaches.

The actual exercise is extremely easy. First, pick a work of art at the museum. I would recommend starting with a representational piece (that is, a painting with identifiable subject matter). Everyone stands in front of the work, but no one reads any of the explanatory material that might be associated with it. You look only at the piece. Then you take turns offering words (or very short phrases) that occur to you as you look. The words may be virtually anything—you need not justify your choice—but you may not repeat a word. That is one of the reasons a pencil and paper come in handy. Someone should write down the words as you go along. If there are only two of you, just go back and forth. The words may be descriptive or interpretive. Pretend we are standing in front of the *Mona Lisa*. Your word list might include "lady, river, mountain, smile, eyes, hands, hair, veil, eyebrows, dark brown, cracks, oil paint, mysterious, gloomy, clear, grin, smirk, depth, nose, folds, dress, line, neck, sky, soft, hazy, shadows, blue, green, uneven, landscape, portrait, old, famous." In a class of 20 students, we go around the room five or six times. With only two or three people, you should still try for as many words as possible—50 or 60 at least. Synonyms are fine—you can use this opportunity to expand the child's vocabulary! You might be surprised at how many words even young children can contribute. When you look at the finished list, you will be amazed at how much it tells you about how you feel about the piece and how much information you have culled from it.

This activity need not end here. The word lists can be used in several ways. For instance, the child could write a poem or story using the collected vocabulary. Or he or she might create a montage. Using a museum copy of the work—a postcard or small poster—or a computer printout of it, the child could cut up the words and glue them around the edges like a frame. Imagine a gallery of such enhanced pictures in a scrapbook or on a wall in the child's room!

Concepts to Discuss: After doing this exercise, you might say to the child, "Looking at the words we have written down, what do you think the artist was trying to say or express? Do you think he or she did a good job?" Look at the title of the work. Does it agree with or even enhance your interpretation?

2. Autobiography

Materials

○ A copy of the questions on page 97

"Autobiography" is an activity that works equally well for those of you trying to inspire greater understanding of art and those who would like to encourage creative writing. You will find it a wonderful way to engage children in viewing portraits. When touring a museum or gallery, you can use this as a terrific opportunity to impress children of all ages with the qualities inherent in good portraiture, or you can use this exercise as a way to inspire the development of a character, or even as the starting point for an entire short story.

While touring the museum, explain that you are going to find a portrait that looks interesting. This might involve defining "portrait" if the child is very young. It would probably be best to let the child choose the portrait himself, as this would indicate that an interaction with the work had already begun. If you have more than one child with you, they might each choose a different piece, or perhaps you might have more than one youngster work from the same piece to show how art may be interpreted differently by different viewers. Instruct the participants to avoid looking at the card or plaque bearing the title, artist's name, and date of completion. Their responses should be based entirely on the visual information intrinsic to the artwork.

Give the child the list of questions. (If the child cannot read yet, ask the questions one at a time.) He is to answer these as if he were the person in the picture. The questions listed below are suggested by the Indianapolis Museum of Art, but these could be modified in endless ways, depending upon your interests or the age of the child. A few alternate suggestions are included.

1. What is your name? How old are you? What year were you born?
2. Where were you born and where do you live at the time shown in this portrait?
3. What do you do for a living?
4. What is your hobby?
5. What is your favorite food? Book? Music?
6. What do you do for fun?
7. What advice did your mother always give you?
8. What one thing would you never, ever do?
9. What one thing would you say to the people of today?

Other questions might include: What secret have you never told anyone? What are you most afraid of? What are you proudest of? Whom do you admire the most? Who are your friends? You can adapt the questions in endless ways to elicit the kind of information you are looking for. To have the most fun, children should be asked to "become" the person in the portrait, with appropriate accents and demeanor.

Concepts to Discuss: I first took part in this exercise with a group of art teachers, and the results were not only illuminating but frequently hilarious. Even self-identified shy people had great success with their presentations. I have never looked at a portrait quite the same way since. (You might discover dramatic abilities in your child of which you were unaware.) It could also be an excellent way of opening a dialogue with your child. Because he is theoretically answering as the person in the picture rather than as himself, he might feel free to offer information that is very revealing. The conversations that occur during and after this activity will depend on what the child discovers in the work that speaks to him. Once again, this exercise could also inspire creative writing.

3. Scavenger Hunt

Materials
○ Postcards of various artworks from the museum you are visiting

This activity is a simple way to add interest and improve attention during a museum visit. If you know in advance that you will be visiting a particular museum, you might make an earlier trip to its gift shop and select several postcards of its artworks. Or you could go online and print some pieces from that venue. If the trip is a spur-of-the-moment decision, perhaps you could start with the gift shop and buy the cards without the child seeing them.

This is a scavenger hunt of sorts. Cut or tear a small bit from each of the postcards or printouts and challenge the child to find the artwork that includes that segment. The older the child, the smaller and more obscure you should make the section. If you are taking more than one youngster with you, you could make it a contest of sorts. However, I would not make it a timed activity but rather one of completion. You don't want the kids racing through the galleries but rather paying close attention to the various artworks to see if they have a match. Explain that they cannot ask anyone about their scrap.

I have added that last suggestion for a reason. I should probably confess that when I first heard of this idea several years ago, I used it during a class trip to the Art Institute of Chicago. On the bus ride north, I divided the children into groups, gave each group a small section of a postcard, and explained the nature of the contest. Of course, I had chosen fairly famous works that they would be sure to see, because our time was limited. As soon as they entered the building, my students went to the nearest museum employees, asked if they recognized the painting and, if so, where it was located. It had not occurred to me to insist that they find the works visually, because I assumed they would understand the "rules" of the game. If your little piece is small enough, this might not matter, but be forewarned!

Concepts to Discuss: You might ask the child how he decided which works of art were correct. Was it the colors? Shapes? Textures? Lines? Brushstrokes? Subject? Hard edges versus soft? This activity can provide a nice introduction to a discussion of the different aspects of the chosen piece (and others as well).

4. Find the Concept

This project does not require any physical materials, but it could require some understanding of art vocabulary. Basically, you are going to choose an element or a principle of art and challenge the child to find artworks that display the chosen concept. For instance, with a very young child, the element might be as simple as a shape—perhaps a circle. Then, as you tour the museum, the child can look for circles in the various pieces. These don't have to be literal circles. The child might find a picture or sculpture with objects placed in a circular arrangement. Perhaps a figure's head has been distorted a bit to resemble a circle. You might find ovals and discuss how ovals and circles are similar. Artists frequently use similar or related shapes to help unify a work. Younger children can also tell when something is symmetrical, so you might focus on all the different kinds of balance that artists use.

You could prepare for the trip to the museum by studying a particular concept and then find works that incorporate that concept. For example, the child could do the quilt project on page 32, select a specific color scheme, and then look for all the pictures or other works that display that color scheme. If you are lucky enough to live near a museum and you visit it often, it would be wonderful to follow each project or group of projects done at home with a trip that focuses on that concept.

Of course, a variation on this theme is to pick a particular work of art and ask the child what elements or principles she recognizes in the piece. But I think the method described above will keep a child more involved throughout the tour.

Concepts to Discuss: You will be exploring a particular element or principle during this activity, but that certainly does not mean you can't discuss any other concept that arises. Depending upon your fluency with the vocabulary, it might be a good idea to read the section on definitions (pages 3–16) very carefully, or even to take the book with you when you go.

5. Write a Poem, Song, Play, or Story

Materials
○ Paper and pencil (optional)

You might want to take notes for this activity, so you should check with the museum to be sure that carrying a pencil and paper is permissible. If your child is very young, you might want to write down what she tells you, but older children can write themselves. If they carry a sketchbook as recommended in the "Everywhere" chapter, this is a perfect use for it. There are several ways you can set up this activity.

One possibility is to decide before you visit the museum which genre you are going to aim for: a poem, a story, a play, or a song. Depending upon the child, the goal may not even be verbal in any way. You may decide that you are going to find a work that inspires no lyrics but only a tune or even a dance.

Helping children to see the connections between the arts is extremely productive, especially if you have a budding musician or dancer or even a gymnast. Nonobjective works can be especially useful for nonverbal interpretation. Does this painting have a rhythm the child can use? Is there a motif that repeats? What tone color would she use to interpret this artwork? ("Tone color" describes the qualities of sounds in music and how they are created.) Could the lines in the piece inspire lines of movement or dance or on a staff? If the chosen genre is writing, a "narrative" work of art may be more fruitful. (Narrative art tells a story of some sort. Picture *Washington Crossing the Delaware*.) Seeing the similarities between visual art and the art or activity the child loves can open whole new avenues of interest. How can the child use the visual arts to enhance the genre of her choice? Conversely, a child who likes art but not writing might be encouraged to broaden her outlook.

After selecting the desired art form, the child should browse the galleries until something strikes her as a likely candidate, and she will then jot down any ideas that occur to her. I would encourage roaming around a bit rather than using the first interesting piece, noting the titles of the works that are possibilities and any thoughts the works inspire. However, if a piece bowls the child over and gets the creative juices flowing, I wouldn't insist upon moving on. A youngster who is a wonderful poet might create several verses about one work or might write one poem each about several pieces. A child with a great imagination might jot down several ideas for many delightful stories and only develop one. Even if she doesn't follow through on a tale, the idea will have been planted, and a new way to view the collection will have been instilled.

Another approach is to find a work and discuss what other art form it suggests to the child. Does she think of a song when she looks at this sculpture? A dance? A story? Why did she choose that genre? Encourage her to write down her thoughts about several pieces from that point of view. You can choose to develop these or not, but it will encourage everyone involved to look at art in a different way.

Another possibility involves a museum game called What Comes Next? This particular approach is a great way to integrate art and drama, although it certainly could yield a story, a dance, or even a song. It would probably be more productive (and fun!) with several children, but one or two youngsters can certainly play.

The concept is very simple. Find a painting, sculpture, or photograph that portrays a person or people doing something. Have the child take a pose as close to the one in the artwork as possible. Once the position is correct, ask the child, "What comes next?" The youngster should then continue the action from that pose on. If several children are participating, imitating a group in an artwork, this can result in some pretty hilarious situations, so you might caution the kids not to get too noisy.

Concepts to Discuss: The topics you discuss will depend largely upon the approach you take to this activity. If you focus on the more nonverbal variations—tunes and dances and so forth—your focus will probably be more on elements and principles, while if storytelling is emphasized, you will talk a great deal about the evocative aspects of various pieces.

6. Which Is Your Favorite? Why?

Perhaps the easiest way to engage a child in a museum visit is to ask a simple question, such as "Which work is your favorite?" And perhaps the more important question, "Why?" Before you go, you could explain to the youngster that each time you enter a gallery, you want him to look at all the pieces and pick his favorite. Then ask him what there is about the work that he especially likes. Once you have discussed why he likes it, you might ask him if he thinks it's a great work. Of course, the question doesn't have to be about his favorite work. It might be something more provocative, such as "Which piece do you really dislike?" followed, of course, by the all-important "Why?" or "Do you think it is well done?" Even young children can have strong likes and dislikes. Stress the fact that he can only choose one piece.

There is an interesting museum game called Token Response. The game comes with colorful cardboard cutouts: green rectangles that stand for money, some blue ribbons, a clock, a heart, a house, and a few others. The game is usually played with an entire class. Each child gets a set of symbols, and she is to put her green token in front of the piece she feels is the most valuable. She should put the clock in front of the work she feels took the longest to make, the heart in front of the one she loves the most, the house in front of the one she would like to have in her home, the blue ribbon in front of the one that she thinks is the best, and so on. These are all thought-provoking avenues to explore and great conversation starters, although some can be discussed for longer periods. You could certainly buy the game, especially if you are accompanying more than one child. The placement of groups of tokens can generate interesting conversations. Was one piece a general favorite? Did many children select one artwork as the best? Did one work get both liked and disliked? You don't have to have tangible symbols to spur conversation. The important thing is to ask questions that cause the child to think about the various works.

Concepts to Discuss: It is important for children to understand that there is a difference between liking and judging. When we say we like something, we don't have to defend our statement. We don't have to prove anything. I might like a portrait because the person in it resembles a beloved uncle or an abstract painting because the artist used my favorite colors. Whenever you start a sentence with phrases such as "I think" or "I believe" or "I like," no one can argue with you. Saying "I believe the sky is red" is not the same as saying "The sky is red." When I say I like a work of art, I may have several reasons for my feelings that have nothing to do with logic, rules of good composition, or great draftsmanship.

But when I state that a work of art is good or bad—when I judge the work—I must defend my judgment with some sort of proof. We all have books or songs or movies that we love, but at the same time, we are aware that they are not great art. They are just very enjoyable. If you do play Token Response, you may find that the child does not always put the blue ribbon and heart by the same piece. A visit to a museum is a great time to discuss the difference between liking and judging.

7. Vanitas Hunt

One of my favorite topics in art history is vanitas symbolism. This is a subject that might be more appropriate for an older child. We explore it in sixth grade when we study the Baroque era, but I introduce it during a museum visit in fifth grade. Your decision might depend upon your child's religious background.

Have you ever seen beautiful Dutch still lifes from the 1600s or 1700s? Exquisite vases of flowers or tables of exotic foods? Or perhaps you have seen paintings of people playing musical instruments. Sometimes a work will include all of these elements. A person playing an instrument might be seated next to a bowl of fruit and some flowers. These visuals are all symbolic, and the people of the time would have been well aware of their meaning.

Imagine a painting of a beautiful vase of flowers. Some of the flowers are in bud, some are just opening, some are full blown, and others are wilted. Perhaps one is even broken off and lying on the tabletop. There might be some stalks of wheat in the arrangement. There could also be a snail on the table and a butterfly or two hovering over it.

The flowers represent the cycle of life. We are born, we mature, we grow old, and we die. They also represent the passage of time in another way. The bud may symbolize spring, the mature bloom is summer, and the wilted flower is autumn. The butterfly represents the metamorphosis from earthly body to heavenly spirit. The snail symbolizes evil that we should avoid—like the serpent after the Garden of Eden, it crawls on the ground. The picture is actually a Christian morality lesson about the transience and brevity of life. It is warning us to pay more attention to the good of our souls than to earthly goods and pleasures.

Such works are called vanitas paintings, probably a reference to a line in the first chapter of Ecclesiastes, part of which reads, "Vanity of vanities, all is vanity. What profit hath a man of his labor...? One generation passeth away, and another generation cometh, but the earth abideth forever."

I should probably add a brief aside here. I am Jewish, but I find vanitas symbolism fascinating. I teach at a very multicultural, multireligious school, and my students also find it fascinating. It is in no way necessary to believe in Christian doctrine in order to appreciate what the artist was saying. I don't proselytize; I interpret. I also teach about ancient Egyptian religion when we study the art of that period, because you cannot fully understand why Egyptian art looks the way it does without understanding the culture that created it. When we study Asian art, we learn about Buddhism, Islam, Confucianism, and Taoism. A great deal of Western art displays Christian iconography, and in order to fully appreciate the artist's message, you have to understand the vocabulary of the work.

There are myriad other symbols in a vanitas painting. Skulls and hourglasses are pretty obvious in meaning, but others are not. Anything associated with bread—wheat, pretzels, loaves—refers to the body of Jesus, while wine represents his blood. Fine materials (crystal, silver, and gold) and exotic foods (figs, dates, and citrus fruits) symbolize the earthly riches that cannot buy one's soul a place in heaven. (Flowers are also a symbol of wealth, especially tulips, which cost a great deal at one time.) Like flowers, foods have a life cycle. They are fresh or partly eaten, and we all know they will eventually rot.

Flowers could have individual symbolism as well. For example, lilies are frequently associated with the Virgin Mary or purity, and many other flowers have meanings that would have been known to the people of the day.

Paintings with musical instruments are frequently vanitas works. Music does not last. Once the notes are played, they fade away—another symbol of transience.

An added feature of such paintings is an item resting precariously on the edge of a table, step, or other similar support. Perhaps it is a knife that is shown part on and part off the table. Or a broken flower that might drop off the surface on which the vase is sitting. These items in danger of falling are arranged to remind the viewer of man's fall from grace in the Garden of Eden.

The symbols are somewhat endless. Crystal and pearls were standard symbols for purity. A pen and ink referred to our vain thoughts. The list goes on and on.

The earlier vanitas works are fairly obvious, but vanitas elements appear in paintings right up to the present day. It can be very enlightening to look for these elements throughout your visit to a museum and try to understand how they affect the artist's message. For instance, you might find pictures of beautiful young men or women with vases of flowers, bowls of fruit, and/or musical instruments. The vanitas element can be there to remind us that our good looks are fleeting and that beauty of character is more important.

You could discuss vanitas symbolism before you go to the museum and then see how many works you find that seem to have such a component. Remember, the whole piece need not be vanitas—there might simply be a bowl of fruit in a corner or a small vase of flowers in the background. Of course, not every vase of flowers or bowl of fruit is a vanitas reference, but you will be surprised at how many may be. Certainly, if the painting is Dutch from the Baroque era, you can be quite sure of its meaning. There are vanitas symbols in works by Pablo Picasso, Édouard Manet, and Max Beckman among many others, and artists to this very day use the device. Perhaps your museum has works by Audrey Flack or Janet Fish. You may not know for sure what the artist intended, but you can at least find possibilities.

Concepts to Discuss: If you find the subject of vanitas interesting, you might do some research on it, either by yourself or with your child. This might very well lead to a discussion of symbolism in general. Such a discussion might prove quite helpful in English class. A great deal of Western poetry and prose is rife with Christian symbolism. You might also research the term "memento mori," which literally translated means "remember your mortality." Memento mori paintings usually contain items related to a specific individual.

Another interesting avenue for discussion is the fact that some researchers feel that the vanitas tradition of painting was begun by women artists. Most women in earlier times were forbidden to draw nude models, and they were frequently criticized for their renderings of the human form. Therefore, the theory goes, the drawing of still lifes became a field heavily populated by female artists. Certainly, there were some extremely successful women painters of this genre. When I first studied art history as an undergraduate, few if any women painters of any era were mentioned in the text, and the notion of vanitas was ignored. Older children, especially girls, might be very interested in learning how women artists have been treated throughout history.

8. Drawing in the Museum

Materials

○ Drawing paper

○ Pencil

Most museums will allow people to sketch in the galleries, but, once again, be sure to check with your particular institution about this before you go. This is a great time for a child to use the sketch diary mentioned in the "Everywhere" section (page 17). If she doesn't have one, then any sketch pad or even pages of loose paper will be fine.

There are very few instructions needed here. Tour the museum and let the child copy whatever images strike her fancy. There could be a theme involved. For example, if the youngster loves horses, you might hunt for paintings and sculptures that include such figures and let the child study those.

Copying the work of a gifted artist can be very instructive. You may have seen someone painting or drawing in a museum before. Art students are frequently allowed to make copies of great works as part of their studies. You can learn a lot about brushwork, color mixing, line quality, and composition by trying to re-create what a master has achieved. Trying to reproduce an exemplary work is a time-honored teaching device. Just as a novice in virtually any field can learn from working with a veteran, a young artist can get a great deal from carefully observing and trying to duplicate the work of a master.

It is also not unusual for artists to do personal interpretations of previous artists' works. Even the great Picasso was known to do such interpretations and to adapt other artists' styles in his work. Perhaps you could suggest that your child do a personal interpretation of a piece at the museum.

Concepts to Discuss: Your child will probably do this project in pencil, with perhaps some colored pencil or crayon enhancements, depending on the rules at your museum. There are several questions that might arise. Why did she choose the image or images she chose? (This question might reveal some hitherto unsuspected interest.) How does the piece translate into pencil? Does the drawing focus more on line than color? If so, how does this affect its impact? What are the main differences between the copy and the original? I'm sure you will think of several more questions when you see the chosen piece.

9. How Would You Arrange Your Museum?

Materials
○ Postcards or printouts of images (optional)

This activity does not require any materials, although you can do a variation with a collection of art images.

Virtually all museums have some sort of rationale to the arrangement of their collections. Many museums use chronology in some way. On the second floor of the Art Institute of Chicago, for example, you can follow a time line of Western art history fairly easily from the Renaissance to the late 19th century and beyond. The artist and/or place of origin also plays a part in most arrangements. Asian art will be located in one area, African art in another. Depending on your child's age, you could discuss the layout of the particular museum you are visiting as you go through it. You might even make this a challenge: can the child figure out what rationale this museum used? (Once again, age is a factor here—you will know your child best.)

The real point of this activity is to find out how your child would arrange her own museum. Can she think of a more interesting way to order the collection? Maybe all portraits would be together, regardless of date or point of origin. Landscapes would be grouped together in another area and still lifes in yet another. Picture a museum where a Chinese wall hanging of mountains hangs next to a Bierstadt! Do all cultures create still lifes?

What if all the pictures with dogs were in the same gallery? What about size? Pictures might get bigger or smaller as you wend your way through the building. What if a time line was used, but place of origin was not a factor? That is, a gallery would display art done in the mid-19th century in China, Japan, India, Kenya, South Africa, the United States, Mexico, France, Germany, and Argentina!

Maybe the museum would be arranged by country or alphabetically by artist. Maybe all sculptures would be grouped together with paintings that used similar subject matter. The point is to discuss the ways in which museums display their works and why that theory works. What could be done differently?

A variation on this activity can be done at home, although it would take a broad range of art images. Perhaps you could build this collection up over time. The images could be postcards, calendar reproductions, or works from the Internet. Or maybe you could find an inexpensive book about art history at a used bookstore. (The more color photos, the better!) Cut the photos out individually, mix them up, and ask the child to arrange them in whatever order seems appropriate for her museum. Each pile could represent a different gallery. If you are a teacher using this volume, this would be a great activity for a class!

Concepts to Discuss: Why do museums arrange their art the way they do? Is there a better way? What do we learn from these arrangements? What might we learn from other methods?

In the City

WHETHER YOU LIVE in a city or are just visiting one, the environment has plenty of opportunities for artistic development. Unfortunately, we usually miss most of them. When we go to a museum, we enter expecting to pay attention; when we walk along a city street, we are oblivious to most of the neighborhood. In fact, we learn from infancy to tune out a great deal of the world around us. It would be overwhelming to truly attend to all the surrounding sights, sounds, and smells. We generally focus on things that are important to us, particularly those that are pretty, unusual, or dangerous. Yet a city is built using the elements and principles of art and is rife with art history, so it is a perfect place to study these subjects. The term "city" is used here to imply any urban location—a small town will work just as well as New York, Chicago, or Los Angeles. In fact, many of these projects could be done at a shopping mall.

A few of these activities require a camera for optimum results. A digital camera would work best, but if one is not available, a disposable camera will do. If using these things is not an option for you, I have included some alternatives.

1. Find a Style

Materials
○ Research materials from the library or the Internet

This activity will take a bit of preparation in the form of research. Start by choosing a specific architectural style from history. There are several styles that would be easy to find. Greek, Roman, Gothic, Romanesque, Renaissance, Baroque, Gothic Revival, Classical Revival, Bauhaus, Art Nouveau, and Art Deco are just a few that come quickly to mind. You might get a large illustrated book on architecture from the library and leaf through it together with your child until something strikes your fancy, although you should avoid styles that are too obscure. If there are major chapters about the style, you are probably OK.

Let's say you choose classical Greek architecture. Almost any volume on this subject will illustrate the three main orders of Greek architecture: Doric, Ionic, and Corinthian. It will also display a triangular pediment. Your research can be as simple or involved as you wish. You might merely look at pictures of the three orders and sketch them, especially the capitals. If you are getting the information online, you might print out the illustrations. The idea is to become familiar with the main aspects of your chosen style, although you want to keep it easy. Look for those elements that are quite obvious. With a very young child, this step might be as basic as choosing a single type of column or a pediment. With older children, depending upon their knowledge base, you might choose something subtler.

You could leave your research at that, or you could go into more depth. You could read about the style and why it represented the culture that created it. You could get other books and go through more illustrations or surf the Web for information on your topic. At the very least, however, the idea is to have a few typical examples to take with you on your trip to town. As stated above, even one Greek order would be fine. Or a pediment. Or a Roman or Renaissance dome. Or the rose window from a Gothic cathedral. Or the floral designs from Art Nouveau or the Egyptian motifs or geometry from Art Deco. Focus on one or two elements.

The next step is very simple. As you stroll around town—your hometown or a vacation spot—look for the elements you have chosen. Some will be ubiquitous. Those Greek columns will pop up everywhere in most cities. You don't even have to be in the heart of town. Most neighborhoods will have houses sporting a column or two. In some cases, the columns will be fairly authentic, with fluting and identifiable capitals. In other cases, they will be somewhat similar, but not identical. You might discuss the differences.

Depending upon your knowledge of architecture and the particular town you are touring, you could steer your child toward a specific style you know is common. Washington, D.C., is bursting with references to ancient Greek architecture, because the Greeks are credited with introducing democracy to the Western world, and our forefathers wanted the new country's capital to be symbolic of our form of government. Many statehouses have classical elements for the same reason. Some cities have wonderful Art Deco buildings because a lot of construction was done in the 1920s and '30s, when this style was popular. Miami Beach is famous for its Deco architecture, and there are also wonderful examples in Los Angeles and New York City. You could research a bit about your town or city and then look for specific examples of the architecture that is mentioned.

This activity is beneficial in a couple of ways. One is historical. History affects us today, especially art history. These aren't dusty old styles that died out long ago. They are reinterpreted and reinvented generation after generation, and designs that are thousands of years old still inspire architects. Also, if you go into a bit of depth during your research, you can sometimes find out fascinating things about previous cultures or the city under discussion and make history come alive for your child.

Of course, the main purpose of the exercise is to cause your child (and you!) to actually observe the chosen town in ways you might have overlooked in the past. I remember finding an Art Deco building in

Indianapolis many years ago. I had passed the structure a number of times, but I had never really seen it. Once I noticed the outside, I went into the lobby and discovered a fabulous set of bronze elevator doors. On another occasion, some of my students went on a class field trip that included a visit to the old post office. Upon their return, they couldn't wait to tell me about the intricate mosaics that decorated the interior of the building. We had just studied Roman art and worked on a paper mosaic project in art class, so they were highly appreciative of the skill and effort involved in the work. I don't think they would have paid the same attention to this aspect of the building without that experience. Once we learn about something, we tend to notice it far more frequently.

Whether you are using this book as a parent or as a teacher, you might look into architectural tours in your town or city. Some towns have volunteers who lead such tours for free. These can be fascinating, especially if your location has hidden treasures. If you are a teacher who has taught architectural styles or perhaps a particular era, such as ancient Greece or Rome, as part of history or art, you might take your students on a general walk around town to see what elements they recognize.

Finally, architecture, like painting and sculpture, can be expressive. A bank or a civic building might be designed to impart a feeling of solidity and permanence. The style for such structures is usually based on traditional models rather than avant-garde designs, even if there are some modern interpretations. A trendy restaurant, on the other hand, might use the latest, cutting-edge styles to imply that what is served inside is like nothing you've eaten before.

Concepts to Discuss: As you walk around the city, do you notice a preponderance of one or two styles? Even if you don't set out to find a particular element, you might notice that the town or neighborhood seems to have a lot of Victorian "gingerbread" or columns and pediments. When was the city founded? What architectural styles were popular during its building booms? Does the town, or at least the area you are in, have a special atmosphere? You might also ask your child how a certain building makes her feel. Does she want to go inside? Does it look safe? Old? New?

2. Look for Different Forms or Shapes

Materials
○ Digital camera and printer (optional)

This is an extremely simple activity you can do with even young children, if they understand the concept of form or shape. They should have a vocabulary of some basic forms, such as cubes, rectangular prisms, spheres, cones, pyramids, and cylinders, or shapes like circles, squares, triangles, rectangles, and octagons. Then, as you walk around town, try to identify as many forms or shapes as possible.

I would make these two separate activities. If you are focusing on forms, restrict your visit that day to forms and do shapes another time. If you are doing forms, rectangular prisms should be everywhere, but finding spheres, cones, pyramids, and cylinders should be a bit more challenging. Don't overlook partial forms. Is the dome on the top of that building truly half a sphere, or is it more ovoid? Aren't those columns skinny cylinders? An "engaged" column might be half a cylinder.

Shapes are far easier, and there will probably be many more of them. Pentagons, hexagons, heptagons, octagons, pentacles, six-pointed stars, semicircles—the day could turn into quite a geometry lesson! These shapes (and the forms noted above) need not be restricted to buildings. Signs, bridges, manhole covers, park benches, trash receptacles—anything in the cityscape is fair game.

If you have a digital camera, this activity can yield some nice photos. The goal is to have at least one photo of each shape or form the child has identified. Digital cameras are best here, because when you are three feet from the stop sign you both believe is the perfect subject for "octagon," you will find a great window that is even better, and digital photos don't waste film. Of course, you can have as many of each shape or form as you want, but you will have to be selective when you print.

I recommend setting the camera on black-and-white so that the focus is truly on the geometry. Zoom in as much as possible, so that the shape or form fills the frame. For very young children, you might take the pictures yourself, but if the youngster is able to handle the camera, the exercise is far more fun.

If you take the child to different cities, this could be a great ongoing project. Imagine a binder with photos of the geometry of each town or a separate pocket folder for each location. Or you could divide the photos by shape or form. The section marked "Circles" could be filled with pictures with titles such as "Indianapolis," "Chicago," and "New York" or "My Neighborhood," "Uptown," and "Downtown." Noticing shapes and forms will cause you and the children to see the urban environment in a whole new way.

Concepts to Discuss: Are certain shapes or forms more common than others? Why? On a recent trip to Shanghai, I was amazed by the fact that so many of the buildings were not rectangular prisms. Much of Shanghai's high-rise architecture was built during the last 18 years or so. Now, each time I visit a city, I look particularly for buildings that are not based upon the usual glass box made so popular by such architects as Ludwig Mies van der Rohe, Walter Gropius, and Le Corbusier in the mid-20th century.

3. Drawing on Photos for Perspective

Materials
- Digital camera and printer or magazine photos of city streets
- Pencil
- Ruler

Although there are alternative ways to do this project, the most productive involves a digital camera and printer. This activity might not work for very young children, but if the youngster can take photos and draw a straight line using a ruler, it should be appropriate. Once again, you will know your child's capabilities best. Also, you might feel more comfortable if you do a little study of basic linear perspective before you begin this activity. Even a cursory glance at a book or website should give you a general idea of the theory behind this concept.

As you tour the city, have the child take photos that stress perspective. One aspect of perspective is that lines that are parallel to the ground seem to merge in the distance at points at our eye level. Our eye level is represented in perspective drawings by a horizontal line called the horizon line. The point on the horizon line at which lines appear to merge is called the vanishing point. If you are looking straight down a long street, the lines will all seem to merge at one point.

If you are standing at a corner looking down both streets, there will be two vanishing points.

"Lines" refers to things such as the tops and bottoms of buildings, the tops and bottoms of windows and doors, sidewalk edges, lane divisions, and so forth. Cars and people will appear smaller as they recede

A photo exhibiting one-point perspective.

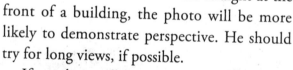

An example of two-point perspective.

into the distance. Our brain will know this is only an illusion, but if something in the distance doesn't appear smaller, our brain will decide it is actually huge.

If the child aims the lens down a street rather than straight at the front of a building, the photo will be more likely to demonstrate perspective. He should try for long views, if possible.

If you have tall buildings, you might have the child stand fairly close to the bottom of one and take a photo looking up.

This angle produces a type of perspective in which vertical lines also seem to vanish to a point in the sky. If you are able to take a picture looking down from a high vantage point, the vertical lines may appear to vanish to a point below you.

I would recommend setting the camera to take pictures in black-and-white or at least printing the photos in black-and-white. Print them on simple computer paper, and make

vanishing point

them fill the page or choose an 8-by-10-inch format. Then let the child draw over the key lines on the photo with a pencil. This step should be done using a ruler. If the lines are covered precisely, they should meet at the vanishing point or points.

If the vanishing point is off the page, you can tape the photos to a larger sheet, like newspaper, to accommodate the longer lines.

Sometimes it is hard for a child to understand what we are talking about when we point to this apparent merging of lines in the real world. This exercise will help them see the concept more clearly. Older children can have a great time taking unusual points of view, although I would encourage them to become comfortable with simple one- and two-point perspective first.

There are fun special effects that can be achieved with perspective. As stated above, people in the distance appear smaller than those up close. You could take some fun shots of the

vanishing point

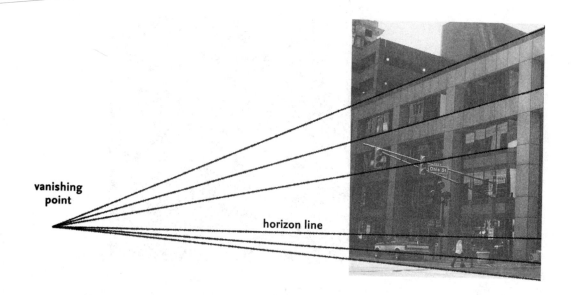

vanishing
point

horizon line

child pinching a friend between her fingers or holding her in the palm of her hand. Or you could be the small person and the child or her friend could take the shot. Kids love these illusions!

There are other ways you can illustrate lines vanishing to a point without a camera. One option is to find pictures of cityscapes in a magazine or newspaper and let the child use those to draw on. Another is to find a large book with city views at the library and use tissue or tracing paper placed over the photos. You can also do this project without going downtown. A view down the side of any building should work, as will long hallways and certain interiors.

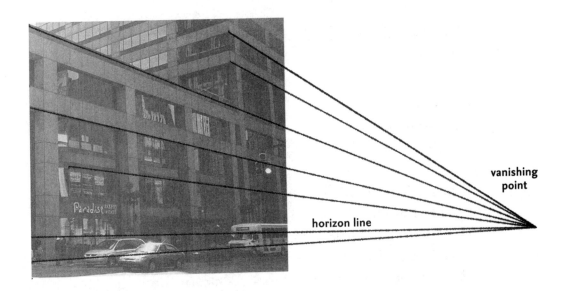

vanishing point

horizon line

Concepts to Discuss: The definition of perspective we use in class is "point of view." We stress that the phrase is not exclusive to art. People have different points of view about politics, religion, history, movies—you name the subject, and someone will "view it from a different angle" than you do. Older students will have studied voices in language arts—a first-person narration versus a third-person one, for example—and different characters certainly have different views of the plot. It is always a good idea to define terms as broadly as possible, to show their applications in other areas. You can also spend a lot of time discussing how a photographer's point of view affects the quality of the shot.

Drawing on Photos for Perspective

4. Finding Letters

Materials
○ Camera (optional)

On a recent trip to New York City, my family and I tried this activity, and we had a terrific time. (I am 63, my husband is 72, and my sons are in their 30s, so people of all ages can enjoy this project.) We all agreed that it caused us to notice the details of our environment in a way we had not done before. It also causes the participants to think about shapes in a whole new light.

The premise is quite simple: you are going to look for letters in the built environment. (Letters on signs, of course, don't count.) As you can see from the photos below, these letters may be found in ironwork, windows, overall structure, or fire escapes—any structural formation. Some will be very easy to spot, but others, like Q and R, might be challenging.

If you have a camera, you can capture the letters and use the photos in a variety of ways. You could print out the letters that spell the name of the city or town and make a sign as a memento of your trip. I would recommend the prints be black-and-white (and the same size, of course) for uniformity. If a letter is repeated, try to find different instances of the shape. You might also highlight the actual letters with a transparent marker. You might spell out your own name or create someone else's as a gift. You might also try to find numbers and create your address.

This activity will work just as well without a camera. List the letters of the alphabet and mark off each one as you find it. Or put a check-mark by each letter every time you find it.

Note: The following photos were taken in downtown Indianapolis, but any small town or group of buildings can provide several—if not all—of the letters of the alphabet.

Concepts to Discuss: This activity helps the participants pay far more attention to the lines, shapes, and forms in our environment. It helps them notice how more complex shapes and forms are constructed from simpler ones. You might also discuss how little notice we usually give to our built environment.

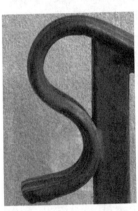  

Don't forget to consider cursive and lowercase letters.

5. Urban Elements and Principles

Materials
○ Camera (optional)

This project could be done on a single occasion, or it could be spread over several visits to a town or city. It could definitely be adapted into a great field trip for an art class.

Your first step is to go over the definitions of the elements and principles in the "Brief Overview" section (pages 3–16). For a younger child, you might limit the project to elements only or even a single element. Later you could do a separate trip for principles. Again you might limit the tour to one principle.

The idea is to find at least one example of each of the elements and/or principles you have chosen as your subject. Let us say you are escorting a very young child, and you have limited your search to shapes. Look for as many different shapes as you can find. If you have a camera, take snapshots of squares, circles, triangles, and other shapes. If you are doing all the elements, the child can look for buildings or signs with strong, bold colors, and take extreme close-up shots of pebbly or rough surfaces. If you don't have a camera (or even if you do!), be sure to feel the surface the child has chosen for texture. Value might be represented by a photo of an area with strong highlights and deep shadows. Line could be illustrated by the cracks in a sidewalk or the muntin bars on a window. Examples of shapes and forms should be a snap to find.

Among the principles, while all of them will be present in some form, you might consider searching for examples of balance as an excellent way to spend an afternoon. Look for all three kinds: formal, informal, and radial. (Hubcaps are prime sources for radial designs.) Children might find a great deal of symmetry, but some formal balance is not quite that exact. Once again, how picky you are with the vocabulary will depend upon the level of the child's understanding.

Pattern is another great subject for a search. Children can try to find regular patterns and random ones and then try to decide which type is more common. Having photos or printouts of your findings would be terrific. Imagine a notebook or a schoolroom wall filled with examples of the elements and/or principles your children have found for themselves.

Concepts to Discuss: What you discuss will depend on the elements and/or principles you choose to focus on in this project. Once again, you might want to review the definitions on pages 3–16.

6. Find Your Favorite Structure

Materials
- ○ A library and/or a computer; a camera (optional)
- ○ Paper
- ○ Pencil

When you give your child a specific purpose for looking around town, he will see things differently than if you merely say, "Isn't this a fine-looking city!" The primary goal of this activity is to cause the youngster to find things that might have escaped his notice otherwise and to think about them.

There are a couple of different ways to approach this exercise. You might specify that the child is to select his favorite building, or you might include other aspects of the environment, such as bridges, sculptures, monuments, or fountains. It somewhat depends upon the nature of your town or city. Let's assume you have chosen to limit the activity to buildings. The actual task is simple: the child is to make notes about buildings he likes or finds interesting in some way, and at the end of the day, he should pick one or two as his favorites.

Of course, there are different ways to make these "notes." He might take a photo of the selected buildings, being careful to write down the address and any other pertinent information. If he doesn't have a camera, he could write down the info and either add a verbal description of the structure or do a quick sketch to remind himself of its design. (This would be a great time to use a sketch diary.) Of course, if you are working with a very young child, you could help with the writing and sketching. Whether you choose buildings, sculptures, fountains, or other artifacts, you will follow the same procedure.

You might decide to simply end the activity at this point. Taking note of the artifacts he particularly likes will certainly make a trip to town more interesting and will cause the child (and you!) to pay closer attention to your surroundings. However, you can take this exercise one step further and select one or two artifacts to research.

If the child chooses a major building, bridge, fountain, or sculpture, his research will probably be fairly easy. You might decide to end the day at the public library, where there will certainly be books about your city's buildings and artifacts. The librarian should be able to help you if you and the child run into any snags. Or you could go home and search the Internet together for the information. If you have a smartphone, you can pull up information as you stand in front of the chosen structure. A lot will depend upon the amount of information available on the site. Does the building, bridge, or fountain have a name? If a sculpture is chosen, is it signed in some way?

There are computer prompts that can get you started. I entered "Indianapolis buildings" into a search engine and found a terrific website that was loaded with information. The key factor in your research success will probably be how "important" the structure is. It will be much harder to find information on a common office or apartment building, but the odds of your child choosing such an edifice are probably slim.

Concepts to Discuss: Be sure to ask your child why he chose the structures he did. Do you see a trend? Does he like older buildings with lots of texture and detail? Does he prefer unusual modern forms? Does he like sculpture more than architecture? Does he like buildings that seem "friendlier"? Remember, sometimes we can't explain why we like something, and we certainly don't have to defend our choices, but if your child can articulate his reasons, it could lead to some interesting insights about his personality.

If you are dealing with an older child, you might initiate a valuable discussion about the difference between liking and judging. If you say you like or dislike something, that is different from saying it is good or bad. For example, if you say, "I thought that movie was great," people may question your taste, but they can't say you are wrong. Only you know what you thought. But if you say, "That is a great movie," that is a judgment, and you must have arguments to back up your assessment.

When you start a sentence with words like "I think," "I believe," or "It seems to me," others can't truly dispute what you say. People frequently like works—movies, songs, TV shows—that they know are not high art. They are not judging them; they are simply enjoying them. The concept of liking versus judging is also covered in project 6, "Which Is Your Favorite?" in the "At the Art Museum" chapter.

7. City Draw and Fill

Materials
- Paper
- Pencil
- Black marker
- Coloring medium (crayons, colored pencils, or oil pastels)
- Digital camera and printer or screen (optional)

This project offers a nice blend of observational realism and imagination. I saw a wonderful art teacher named Kay Clay do a similar activity when I was in college.

The first step will be for the child to select a subject. This could be a building (or even part of one), a bridge, a monument, a bench—virtually any urban subject will do. The more ornate, the better. That is, something like a church facade with a rose window will work better than a simple glass tower.

There are several ways to proceed, depending upon how much time you have. If you are in a rush and have a digital camera, you might take a photo of the subject and do the actual project later. If time allows, step one is to do a pencil line drawing based on the chosen object. This need not be absolutely accurate, but it should closely resemble the subject when it is complete. This part of the activity involves observational drawing. Remind the child to create outlines only—nothing should be filled in. Once again, you could stop and take the project home to finish, or do the next step on-site.

When the pencil drawing is complete, step two requires the child to carefully trace over the pencil lines with a black marker. A regular marker will work better than a skinny one, although you should caution the child to use the point and not the side of the felt nib. For this particular project, the lines should be contour lines, not sketchy or messy. Think of the lines in a coloring book.

Up to this point, the drawing has been highly realistic. Step three should be extremely creative. Oil pastels are best for this step, but any colored, dry medium will do. If you used indelible marker, even wet media, like watercolor, could be added. The idea is to fill each of the shapes on the page with brilliant hues (without white or black). Reality is not an issue here. If there is sky in the picture, it can be red or yellow. Gray bricks could be blue or orange or purple. The color choice should be as bold and fanciful as possible. Whatever medium the child is using should be applied richly for the most expressive effect, although he should try to stay off the black marker lines. If you want to use markers for all the coloring, fill in the shapes before going over the pencil lines with black. See the color illustration on page C-7.

The illustration need not include a huge portion of the subject.

Concepts to Discuss: Since this activity is a combination of realism and expressionism, it would offer a great opportunity to discuss the fact that artists can approach subject matter from different perspectives. Sometimes they use a mimetic approach. That is, they try to mimic what they see—to create a realistic representation of the subject matter. Sometimes they produce a version of the subject that is more expressive. They might use exaggerated lines or colors or shapes that infuse the work with emotion. Last, they might reduce the subject matter to its simplest shapes or create a very rational design from it. We call this approach formalism. See the discussion of styles on pages 14–15. Even if you don't go into much detail, it is important for children to understand that art is not always realistic in nature.

Another nice discussion could be based on a comparison of the picture before and after the color is added. You might also comment on the colors the child chooses. Are they mostly warm colors? Cool? Primaries? Secondaries?

City Draw and Fill

8. How Would You Draw These Noises? Smells?

Materials

○ Sketch diary (optional)

This project is extremely adaptable. The entire activity might be a discussion as you tour the town. Or it might result in actual artwork—either on-site or back at your home. The sketch diary recommended in the "Everywhere" section would come in very handy here for jotting down ideas and visual notes.

The concept is quite simple. As you walk or drive around, you will hear noises and smell aromas (hopefully nice ones!). How would you express these sights and smells artistically?

For instance, imagine you are walking past a bakery, and wonderful fragrances are wafting out into the street. Ask your child how she would draw or paint those particular aromas. What colors would she use? Would there be lines? If so, would they be straight or curvy? Light or dark? What shapes come to mind? Perhaps the smells bring a particular scene to mind, but the image will probably be extremely abstract. All of these ideas should be jotted down in the sketch diary if the child brought it. Depending on the age of the child, these notes can be very simple. If a box of crayons or colored pencils is available, notes can be very visual in nature. As the child breathes in the wonderful smells, what colors does she want to pull from the box? What kind of lines or shapes will she draw?

This process can be repeated with other smells and sounds—horns honking, sirens wailing, people talking, music from a store, church bells, aromas from an Italian or a Chinese restaurant. Don't overlook unpleasant smells—tar, garbage, or car exhaust—or unpleasant sounds—people shouting, babies screaming, or brakes screeching. In the interests of time, you might suggest at the beginning of the outing that you will pick a favorite sound or smell. Or, if time is not a factor, you can stop whenever a particular fragrance or noise impresses you.

Once your trip is over, you can end the activity, or you can encourage the child to create an actual artwork when you return home. Here, again, are several possibilities. The child might make a drawing or painting that expresses a single experience, or she might create a work that merges all the sensory impressions she received on her trip. The medium can be virtually anything—collage, paint, crayon, colored pencils, markers—and the work can definitely be abstract.

Concepts to Discuss: The obvious subjects for discussion are outlined above. However, you might also consider discussing the difference between realism and expressionism. These concepts are discussed in the previous activity and on pages 14–15.

9. Reduce Scenes to Shapes and Lines—Simplify

Materials
- Paper and pencil or camera (optional)
- Markers, crayons, cut paper, paints, or colored pencils (optional)

This activity can be done with a wide variety of media: pencils, markers, crayons, cut paper, paints—virtually any materials could be used to interpret the sketches you make or the photos you take. This is another great opportunity for the child to use his sketch pad to make drawings and notes.

The focus of this exercise is to abstract shapes and lines from the environment. You might decide to start with a camera. If this is the child's only tool, he takes pictures of streets and buildings, signs and monuments, and telephone poles and newsstands. The actual project will be done at home. It would be very helpful to print the photos out. (If you are doing this on your personal printer, use plain paper and print in black-and-white. There is no need to waste money on this step.) Then he reduces the scene to its basic shapes and lines. Encourage him to eliminate unnecessary details—the idea is to focus on fundamental structure and create a nice composition. He can certainly zoom in on an area—the picture does not need to be used in its entirety. The basic drawing should be done in pencil on paper, but the ultimate project could be finished in a variety of ways.

The child can finish the piece with crayon or marker or colored pencil. The work could be the inspiration for a

painting in acrylics on canvas or tempera on paper or cardboard. The drawing could even inspire a collage. If colors are added, they can be extremely fanciful or very expressive of the feelings inspired by the urban experience.

If time allows and the child has his sketch diary with him when he is in the city, he can start simplifying on the spot. Looking at a street scene or a particular building or structure, he can make drawings that simplify what he is observing. Once again, however, the final project will be completed at a later time. And in both cases, whether he is working from reality or from a photo, you will be encouraging him to find the basic shapes in the subject. Rectangles should be abundant, but many other shapes will appear as well. Lines may occur in the form of telephone wires or exterior electric cables. It can be very difficult to stay focused on the main shapes and not be distracted by all the details, but looking beyond the surface of things is a skill artists should develop.

Concepts to Discuss: As stated above, learning to see the basic structure of things is extremely important to an artist. This skill is useful to other professionals as well—engineers and architects come to mind. But you might very well expand upon this concept. We all get distracted by what we might call surface details in daily life and lose sight of the basics. A composer must have a strong underlying composition before she worries about adding unusual synthesized sounds to the piece. If an author doesn't have a strong plot or character, using fancy words won't hide that fact. A house may look fabulous on the outside, but if it is poorly constructed, it won't last—or at best it will cause a lot of problems for its owners. We could even carry the analogy into the way we live our lives. The possibilities for a meaningful discussion are virtually endless. A great deal of what we learn in art has broader implications.

10. Write a Poem, Song, Play, or Story

Materials
○ Pencil and paper or sketch diary

If you have not already done so, read "Write a Poem, Song, Play, or Story" in the "At the Art Museum" chapter (page 100). The theory is exactly the same—only now the child will have much more sensory input to inspire him. Perhaps the beauty or dilapidation of a particular building will stir him. Or the sounds of traffic. Or the smells of a bakery or restaurant. Perhaps his play, song, story, or poem will be based upon his entire experience. Maybe you have gone into town for a particular reason—an ice show or lunch or a movie—and that event is what motivates him to create. This is a wonderful opportunity to make entries in his sketch diary, and doing so will cause him to notice things around him that he might otherwise overlook.

Concepts to Discuss: As in the museum version of this activity, the nature of the discussion that ensues will rely on the genre of art form chosen (music, poetry, story, or play) and the particular object or experience chosen as the stimulus. Perhaps the child chooses the sound of traffic upon which to base a song. You might discuss instruments, rhythms, and motifs. Each situation will offer a different approach to vocabulary.

11. Photo Blowups

When I went downtown to take the photos for some of these projects, I accidentally discovered another great way to inspire artworks. I was using the camera in my cell phone, and I wanted to review some of my shots. On my particular phone, tapping the screen enlarges the subject. Suddenly, instead of a normal street scene including a streetlight, I found myself looking at an extreme blowup. Only a small section of the enlarged photo could appear in my screen, and that section looked exactly like a work of modern art!

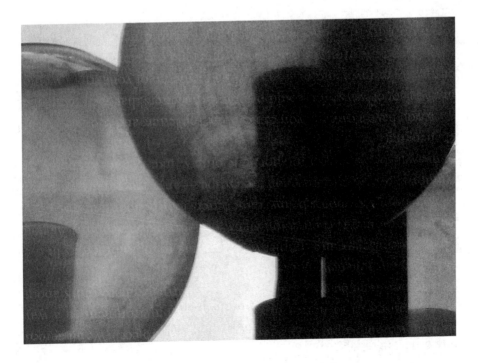

My seventh graders do a project with a similar sensibility. They can use a cropped version of an actual object to create a formalist composition. But this photographic approach can be much simpler.

There are several ways you can complete this project. If you are using a digital or cell-phone camera, you can zoom in on your photo very easily. Many children are old enough to manipulate this gadgetry themselves. Others may need a parent's help. Scan the enlarged areas of the photo until an interesting composition appears. Once the child has the chosen section on the screen, he or she can use the image to inspire a drawing.

For those of you with computers and photo-manipulation software, you could download the picture and crop the section you want to use. The child could then draw from the image on the screen, as in the above scenario, or print out the cropped section.

A third alternative involves a very old-fashioned approach. Print out a copy of the photo and use two L-shaped cutouts to locate an appropriate section.

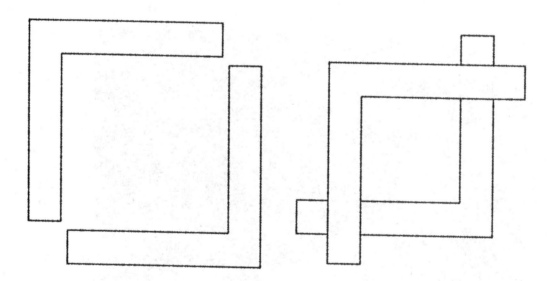

Once the pencil drawing or printout is complete, it can be used to inspire a more complete artwork, one using markers, crayons, paint, or any other materials.

Concepts to Discuss: Hunting for the best composition could lead to a great discussion about what makes good design. Are the elements balanced? Is there color involved? Look for interesting distortion in close-ups of windows. Do those wiggly areas look cool next to the geometric ones? Why does the child like one section of the picture more than another? Why do you?

At the Park

T**HE TERM "PARK"** is used loosely here. This could be an actual park, a rural area, the beach, a camping vacation, or even your own backyard—anywhere you have access to trees, sand, dirt, rocks, grass, and other natural subjects.

1. Trace and Rub Leaves

Materials
- ○ Various leaves
- ○ Paper (not too heavy—computer paper is fine)
- ○ Crayons
- ○ A smooth, even surface (a table, drawing board, or piece of cardboard)

In my curriculum, I use this project to introduce the elements of art. If you are dealing with a very young child and you wish to introduce the elements, you might want to explain the nature of an element. I usually say something like, "Elements are the basic building blocks of our world, and each subject has its own elements. In science, these are the actual elements, such as oxygen, carbon, or hydrogen. Water can be broken down into hydrogen and oxygen. Music has elements like harmony, rhythm, and tempo, while literature has character, plot, and setting." Elaborate as much as necessary to get the point across. If you are working with an older child, you might want to point out the fact that an artist drawing a leaf realistically needs to pay attention to all the elements—color, shape, texture, value, line, and form—and let it go at that.

The youngster can gather the leaves himself, although he might need help reaching some. You could also check to be sure that the ones he chooses are not too fragile and that the veins stick out strongly on the "underneath" side. If you want to gather the leaves outdoors but work inside, you can keep them in a plastic bag, and if they are going to sit for a few days, place a slightly damp paper towel in the bag.

If you do want to introduce the elements, try the following. Hold up two leaves of approximately the same size but very different species. Make sure the "top," or darker green, side is facing the child. Ask the following questions: "If I am an artist trying to draw a realistic picture of these leaves, what is the most noticeable difference between them? How would you know which is which?" The answer, of course, is their shapes. Shape is an element of art. "How else could I make the leaves look realistic? How would we know they are not fall leaves?" They are green. Green is a color, and color is an element of art. Point to the stem and veins and ask how you would add them. Elicit the word "line." Ask the child to pick up a leaf and gently stroke both the top and the bottom. What is different? Feeling or texture is another element of art. Hold up your two leaves again. Turn one so that the underside is facing out. Ask the child to describe the difference. They are both green, but one is lighter than the other. In art, we call the use of light and dark value. Draw a simple leaf shape on a piece of paper and try to pick it up. Of course you can't, because it has no depth or thickness—it is only a shape. The real leaf, on the other hand, has three dimensions, or form, so you can pick it up. Form is our sixth element.

Suggest that the child use rubbings and tracings of the leaves to create an artwork. Even very young children have usually had experience with these techniques. If not, you can demonstrate. Place a leaf on a piece of paper and carefully trace around it with a crayon. Then, looking closely at the leaf, draw in the veins. This could be done realistically or in a way that creates a design. Then place a leaf under the same paper and rub over it firmly—but not too hard—with a crayon. Make sure you cover the whole leaf. This crayon can be the same you used for the tracing, or it can be a different color. The leaf can also be the same or different. The child can fill whole pages with a variety of techniques or do different approaches on different papers. My only strong recommendation is that anyone doing this project use dark crayons. Avoid pinks and yellows, especially for the rubbings.

In art, rubbing is technically called frottage. If you have older children, you might use the term. You can adapt this project to older kids in a variety of ways. You might focus on a more sophisticated composition, or have the youngster do a very realistic rendering, or turn the entire project into an abstract design. The results of the basic activity will definitely display color, line, texture, shape, and value, although admittedly form is only implied. If you have time, perhaps you could have the child include cutouts of the leaves that are slightly curled or crumbled.

Concepts to Discuss: The concepts you discuss will depend on how you use this project, but it should elicit the concepts of color, shape, texture, value, line, and form. See the section titled "A Brief Overview of Elements, Principles, and Other Terms" (page 3) for some quick definitions.

2. Fall Trees

Materials

○ Paper

○ Crayons or colored pencils

In Indiana, where I teach, we have some brilliant displays of fall foliage. Depending on your location, you might have to adjust this project, perhaps using ripening fruit or photos.

If you do have an autumn with changing leaves, you might discuss the process with your child. (This would be a nice time for a little science lesson. As the trees lose their chlorophyll—a green pigment—the actual color of the leaves starts to show.) Depending on the age of your child, you might ask some of the following questions: "Why do the leaves change? Do the leaves change suddenly? Do you go to bed one night with green trees and wake up the next morning to see orange, red,

A fall tree created from mixed colors looks far different from one drawn with one crayon.

and yellow? Of course not. The process occurs gradually." You might have older children explain the process to you.

The point of this project is to focus on the creation of fall colors and the gradual way they emerge. Crayons work very well for this project, but colored pencils are fine, too. I would not use markers.

Have the child select a nicely turning, leafy tree and draw it, coloring the crown green. He should not press so hard with the medium that the green is waxy. Then, selecting orange, he should start shading in from one side. Then he can go over the area with increasingly reddish crayons. Now, have the child draw another tree and color the crown of this one with an orange or red-orange taken directly from the box. There is a huge difference. (See illustration in the color section, page C-8.)

Once you have pointed out the possibilities of mixing colors, have the child draw and color the trees around him using the colors that he sees as inspiration. Encourage experimentation. Perhaps a tree is a color straight out of the box. Certain trees turn a pure orange-yellow by late autumn, but even those could usually use a hint of yellow-green or maybe a bit of orange in some spots. Explain that sometimes artists want things to look more realistic and sometimes they want to use color more expressively. You might ask the child to create a work that expresses fall. It can be representational or abstract. If it is abstract, it might focus on the colors of this time of year.

Concepts to Discuss: This project represents a fine opportunity to discuss color mixing in general and the interesting variations that you can achieve. I use a similar lesson to focus on tertiary colors. You could look for all the color mixes the child creates—secondaries, intermediates, and tertiaries. You might also encourage him to mix colors to get the brown of the trunk.

3. Match Using Only Red, Yellow, and Blue

Materials

○ Paper and pencil

○ Red, yellow, and blue crayons, colored pencils, or other media that can be blended

○ Black marker (optional)

This project is a challenging way to introduce or reinforce the concept that primary colors can make all the other colors. Before I explain the activity, I would like to elaborate a bit about the colors themselves.

When we hear someone say "red," most of us probably think about something akin to the color we see on a fire engine or children's toys—what some refer to as true, primary red. Any box of crayons will have one that is labeled "red," and it is perfectly fine to use that crayon for this project. In reality, however, artists understand that there are several reds—some warm and some cool. They are primaries in the sense that no other colors can be mixed to make them. These are colors with names like alizarin crimson and magenta. In Crayola's larger boxes of crayons, you can find magenta, which is a cool, somewhat pinkish-looking red. If you have both the regular red and a magenta crayon (or colored pencil), that's great. If not, either one will do.

The same is true for blue and yellow. There are warm and cool versions of these as well. The difference in yellow crayons is not worth worrying about, although the yellow in the box that Crayola produces for working on construction paper will produce much brighter greens when mixed with blue. So will the regular crayon they call lemon yellow. In blues, you can really see the contrast. If you draw or paint with ultramarine blue, it looks blue. If you draw or paint with cobalt or cerulean blue, it just looks blue. But if you place cobalt next to ultramarine, the ultramarine will look purplish and the cobalt will look greenish. When you mix a warm blue with a warm red, you get a different purple from the one you get by mixing cool with cool or warm with cool.

If I haven't confused you thoroughly with the above explanation, you will be able to do this very simple project. The child is going to do an observational drawing of the landscape around him with pencil and color the piece using only the primary colors. If you have red and magenta, use them both. The range of colors you can create will be much larger. If you have blue and a warmer blue, that's great as well. Crayola labels their green-blue as cerulean, but it is not truly a primary. The crayon they call sky blue seems far more appropriate. You will want to provide plenty of practice paper so that the child can try a mix before actually putting it on the real project. Encourage him to color a bit more lightly with the darker hues. It's hard to make purple, for instance, if you have laid down a waxy layer of blue. Trial and error on the experimental papers will be very educational. Encourage the child to completely fill the space. Of course, colors can be used as themselves, but encourage mixing whenever possible.

Most children learn the basic color mixes in kindergarten. You might want to review the obvious ones: red and yellow make orange, red and blue make purple, and blue and yellow make green. Since it is very difficult to get true secondaries with crayons, most two-color mixes will result in some sort of intermediate. Have the child try mixing all three hues to make various brownish or dull colors. See page C-8 in the color section.

A nice variation on this project is to go over the pencil lines carefully with black marker before adding the crayon. You

This tree was drawn using only red, magenta, blue, sky-blue, yellow, and lemon-yellow crayons.

Match Using Only Red, Yellow, and Blue

might start out with something simpler to focus on—a single leaf or a flower, for example—but any nature subject will work.

Concepts to Discuss: Although this is essentially a color-mixing project, you may end up discussing the shapes or lines on the child's page or his composition. However, it is a wonderful opportunity to focus on primary, secondary, and intermediate colors; warm and cool colors; and even browns and tertiaries. (Check the section on definitions for more information about these terms.)

4. Sand-casting

Materials

- ○ Plaster of paris
- ○ Sand
- ○ Water
- ○ Sand toys or molds (optional)
- ○ Plastic bucket
- ○ Paper clip (optional)

Plaster of paris is a relatively inexpensive medium that can be obtained from almost any craft or hardware store. If this is a problem, there are recipes online for homemade substitutes. One uses flour instead of plaster. I have never used this version, so if you plan to do so, I would make a little bit and let it harden before doing the project. You want a material that truly sets up solidly.

This project requires an area of sand. This would be a great activity to do at a beach, but a sandbox in your backyard or at the local playground will work just as well. You also need water. If you are at the shore or at home, getting it shouldn't be a problem. If you are at a playground, you might check to be sure there is a water fountain or other source of water before you begin.

The activity is to create a sand casting. The first step is to use the sand to create a mold into which the artist is going to pour the plaster.

You will probably want to wet the sand so that it will retain the contours the child creates. Remember, the artist is going to dig down into the sand, creating a negative space into which the plaster will be poured. You might want to start out with a hollow about the size of half a grapefruit. Imagine the result you would get if you pushed the fruit into the damp sand and removed it. Of course, the child will want the form to be a bit more interesting, but there are many objects you might press into the sand to achieve an exciting negative form.

The easiest way to get the appropriate space is to just create it by hand. The child digs out the sand and presses her fingers down further to create what will be the surface of the sculpture. If you have sand toys, you might have a mold of a fish or a seashell. The child can use molds by pressing the convex side down into the sand. The bottom of the bucket could be used to start the form. Press it an inch or two into the sand and then embellish the resulting form.

Once she has the mold she wants, mix the plaster according to the directions on the package. If you are using the ocean as your water source, be aware that the salt content might cause the plaster to harden more quickly. Pour the plaster into the mold and let it set. If you plan to hang the result, you can place a paper clip about halfway into the plaster as it hardens.

When the plaster is completely set, lift it out of the hole and brush off any excess sand. Don't brush off too much. You want a nice coating of sand on the surface of the sculpture, but not so much that it obscures the form. If you embedded a paper clip in the drying plaster, the child now has a memory of the beach or playground to hang on her wall. If not, she has a paperweight.

Concepts to Discuss: Form is the key issue in this activity, but the results will also exhibit texture and shape. The whole topic of sculpture could also be addressed. In one sense, this process does not produce a complete sculpture in the round, but rather a very high bas-relief, at least if hung on a wall. One might argue that, if set on a table, it is a very short sculpture.

5. Rock Sculptures

Materials
○ Relatively smooth rocks
○ Model paint and small brushes or permanent markers

I had a lot of fun doing this project many years ago. My husband and I were visiting friends at a lakefront cottage in Michigan. The shore was rocky rather than sandy, and we spent many hours searching for Petoskey stones. This quest requires a close scrutiny of the rocks, and I began seeing faces in some of the stones. That is, the forms of certain rocks suggested facial features—some smiling, some scowling, some young, some old. I collected a few, and each evening I would spend some time painting the rocks to create the characters I had envisioned. I used the tiny jars of paint you buy at hobby stores for coloring models, but permanent markers and/or paint pens would work as well. You would only need white (for teeth and eyes) and black, although red would be a nice addition. (I created lady rocks with bright lipstick.) These markers and pens, available at craft and hobby stores, are relatively inexpensive, and children could control them much more easily than the brushes required for the model paint. If buying such markers is not possible, a regular black marker will be fine, although it will not be permanent.

You will need to find an area where smooth stones are abundant. This is usually near some sort of water, but such stones might be found almost anywhere outdoors, although you might need to clean some specimens. Encourage the child to look at the form of the stone carefully. Does that protrusion look like a nose? An ear? Does that crack or crease look like a mouth? Can he see a face? If not a human face, what about an animal? Once he sees a visage on the rock, he merely draws in the features more clearly with the markers.

Just finding an appropriate stone can take quite a while. And the child certainly isn't limited to faces. Maybe a stone looks like a whole animal or person or something else entirely.

I occasionally added a step to this activity. I found some small, relatively flat pieces of wood along the shore and glued certain rocks onto them. This created the illusion of a conversation among my characters. This also made it possible to hang the work. However, individual pieces make great little sculptures or paperweights even without that added feature.

Concepts to Discuss: While form is the focus of this project, observational skills and the development of a critical eye are certainly enhanced by this activity. If you are discussing form, you might introduce or reinforce the nature of organic forms.

6. Drawing Trees

Materials
- ○ Pencil
- ○ Paper or a sketch diary

If your child has a sketch diary, this would be a great time to use it. If not, regular paper is fine.

The instructions for this project are extremely simple: go outside and draw trees. It is actually a great opportunity to do observational drawing. In order to get the most out of this activity, it is better to choose a tree with fewer leaves, one where you can see the branches clearly. Small saplings are good subjects.

Your part of this process is very basic: bring the child and the materials to an appropriate venue, explain the purpose, and give the youngster time to draw. However, even if you have little or no art background, you can help your child by pointing out the basic structure of trees. Young artists have a tendency to overlook certain facts about branches, the most important being that, when limbs sprout or divide, the resulting limbs are narrower than the lower ones.

They also frequently draw branches that bulge or look like thorns. Even older children often don't notice the true structure of branches.

this

not

You might point out that the opposite edges of limbs are relatively parallel and that they divide or sprout until the result is small enough to end. They don't suddenly stop or pinch together.

Regardless of the details you point out, the child should be encouraged to draw what she sees, not what she knows. One of the main benefits of observational drawing is to really see the subject.

Observational drawing of natural subjects can be done virtually anywhere using almost any model. In that same park, are there flowers? Weeds? Fallen leaves? Vines? Do you go to zoos or aquariums? What if the child filled pages of his sketch diary with drawings of land animals or fish?

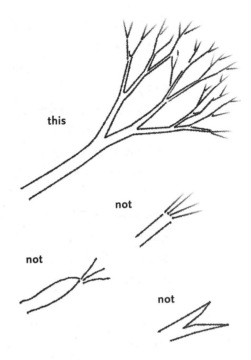

this

not

not

not

Concepts to Discuss: While you may certainly mention the lines, shapes, textures, or values of the chosen subject, the real point of this activity is observation—learning to look. It is more productive here to gently call attention to various details the child may have missed.

7. Prose/Poetry/Play/Music

Materials
○ Pencil and paper or sketchbook

If you have not already done so, read the chapter entitled "Write a Poem, Song, Play, or Story" in the "At the Art Museum" section, page 100. The theory is exactly the same, only now the child will have different sensory input to inspire him—perhaps the beauty or fragrance of a flower, the warmth of the sunlight, the sound of birds. The fluffy clouds floating overhead or the babbling of a brook. The feel of grass under bare feet. Perhaps his play, song, story, or poem will be based upon his feelings about the entire day.

It would be terrific if the child could write stories or poems or songs about all three venues for which this activity is suggested: town, museum, and park. Then the results could be compared. Does music composed to reflect the stimuli found in a town sound different from music based upon a painting or time spent in a forest? Is one area more inspiring to the child than another? This is a wonderful opportunity to make entries in his sketch diary, and doing so will cause him to notice things around him that he might otherwise overlook.

Concepts to Discuss: If the child has already done this activity in another venue, you could discuss the differences or similarities in the outcomes. Talking about the factors that the youngster finds inspiring could be very revealing. Was the city more stimulating for a composer than the park? Was a narrative painting easier to interpret in poetry than the song of a bird? Did colors change drastically? Were certain rhythms similar?

8. A Naturalist's Diary

Materials

○ Sketch diary or paper
○ Pen and pencils
○ Colored pencils
○ Book that identifies local trees and plants
○ Camera (optional)

This activity is a lovely way to combine a little science, writing, art, and observation. Essentially, the child is going to become a naturalist for the day. Many naturalists have produced wonderful paintings and drawings throughout the years. Think of John James Audubon.

You will need some basic materials for this project. The type of sketch diary described in the "Everywhere" chapter (pages 17–27) would be the ideal tool, but any kind of paper will do. You might even use the lined paper that is intended to fit in a three-ring binder. A pen is also a good idea, especially for older children, but a regular pencil is fine. Colored pencils are a must, as is access to a book that identifies the trees, flowers, and other plants that might be found in the area.

Naturalists make certain notations in their journals. If you want to pursue this idea more fully, there are many books and websites that outline the proper procedure. But even if you do not follow strict naturalist guidelines, there are a few notations you should encourage the child to put on each page. What is the date and time? What is the location? What is the weather like? What kind of area are you observing (woods, pasture, wetland, bird sanctuary, park, or backyard)? What season of the year is it? This activity will probably work best when leaves are available. You might discuss these questions with your child and encourage him to jot down the answers at the top of the page. This type of information can be written in pen.

As you walk around the area, you will find trees, flowers, weeds, and bushes. The idea is for the child to make sketches and notations about the vegetation that he encounters. You can certainly include animals as well. Perhaps his first stop is a tree. He can draw a picture of a leaf and an idea of the bark. A younger child might trace the leaf and draw in the veins, using colored pencils to finish the sketch. Is the bark very smooth or rough? Perhaps there are nuts or fruit on the tree. What is the general shape of the tree? Is it large or small, young or old? Can he match the colors? If the child is small, you might write his comments for him, letting him do the sketches. If you have access to a book on local vegetation, the child could try to find the name of the tree or bush and note it in his journal. Many naturalists even draw the clouds on the day they are documenting. Actually, anything that inspires the child is valid subject matter. If you visit such locations often, it would be wonderful to have a sketchbook dedicated only to this type of information.

Concepts to Discuss: If you are a teacher, this would be a terrific opportunity to combine art and science. If your school has trees or some type of garden area, you could work right on campus. If you are at an urban school, perhaps there is a park nearby.

Whether you are a teacher or a parent, you can discuss the many ways in which people in various fields use art. Computers would be pretty boring if people didn't use art in their web designs. Car manufacturers must consider the looks of the car—its form and color, the textures of the interiors—when they produce an automobile. In spite of advances in digital photography, there are still medical illustrators. Advertising would be very ineffective without an understanding of the elements and principles of design.

A former student of mine recently entered dental school. She took her art portfolio with her to her admission interviews. The admissions officers were impressed, because they agreed that there are a lot of aesthetic considerations in dentistry, for example sculpting a crown and matching the color to the patient's other teeth. You might have a little contest to see who can list the most careers that involve art in some way.

9. How Would You Interpret Smells, Sounds, and Feelings?

Materials
○ Sketch diary (optional)

This is essentially the same activity that is described in project 8 in the "In the City" section—"How Would You Draw These Noises? Smells?" (page 130)—so you should read that before proceeding. The only difference will be the types of sounds and scents. Even some of those might be similar. If you are in a public park, you might hear babies crying or people shouting. If your area is more secluded, you will be dealing with the rustling of undergrowth, the breeze in the trees, the sounds of birds and crickets, the smell of flowers or fall leaves or pine sap.

The instructions are exactly the same as the city activity. What colors or shapes or lines would your child use to represent these sounds and smells? What would the resulting artwork look like?

Concepts to Discuss: If you could manage to do both activities, it might be extremely interesting to compare the two resulting artworks. If the activities are limited to notes in the sketch diary, you can compare those. Is there a difference? Were both experiences noisy? Was the rural outing calmer than the urban one? Does this show in the colors and lines and shapes that were chosen? Was one day warm and one cool? Did this affect the elements that were selected?

10. Snow Creatures and Sand Castles

Materials
- ○ Snow or sand
- ○ Sticks, stones, carrots, hat, scarf for snow creatures (optional)
- ○ Plastic buckets or other molds for sand castle (optional)

I realize that this activity is somewhat limited, although at the time of this writing (the winter) practically anyone in the country could build a snowman! Sand castles might be a little harder. Actually, what is important is not so much the activity itself but the idea that common hobbies and pursuits can be viewed as opportunities to discuss elements and principles of art as well as other aspects of the subject. Instead of a snowman or a sand castle, this might apply to a structure made out of Legos, wooden building blocks, or even a house of cards.

I am not suggesting that every time you observe your child engaged in an enjoyable creative pursuit you offer a pedantic lecture. I am merely pointing out that at such times, it is extremely easy to throw in a vocabulary word or two when admiring the product. "What a great snowman!" you might say. "I like the way you used gradation when you made the main parts." Or "What a lovely organic form! See how it flows." Or "The face of your snowman is so expressive—he looks very happy!" Or at the beach, "I love the way those rounded turrets at the corners of your castle contrast with the straight walls! It looks very medieval." When art terms are incorporated into the child's daily life, they become a natural part of her vocabulary. If she asks you the meaning of a word, so much the better! You could also use playing in the snow or in the sand as an opportunity to think outside the box. Does a statue made from snow always have to be a snowman? What about looking at the sculptures of Henry Moore and trying to create a beautiful organic form?

Concepts to Discuss: This activity is really all about discussion. Be sure you are familiar with the art definitions in the "Brief Overview of Elements, Principles, and Other Terms" chapter.

11. Andy Goldsworthy

Materials
○ Books of Andy Goldsworthy's work or visuals from a website
○ Camera (optional)

Andy Goldsworthy is a wonderful artist who uses nature to create his works. It is important that the child see examples of his art before she visits the park or green space. Your public library will probably have one or two of the beautiful books featuring Goldsworthy's work, and there are several websites that can help as well. Aside from his home page, www.morning-earth.org/ARTISTNATURALISTS/AN_Goldsworthy .html is a very nice site. Once you have viewed his creations, the idea behind this activity should become obvious.

This project can be done on a wide variety of levels. A small child could arrange pebbles in interesting shapes or lines, while an older child could use leaves or dandelions or large grasses to create something far more sophisticated. If you have a camera, you or the youngster could take photos of the finished pieces, much as Goldsworthy does. One of the benefits of this activity is that it causes the artist to notice details in the natural world around her.

Concepts to Discuss: The possibilities for discussion during this project are practically endless. Beginning with elements and principles, the child's work will certainly exhibit color, value, shape, line, texture, and form. Many of Goldsworthy's works involve radial balance. There will be repetition, motifs, contrast, gradation, and emphasis. You might wish to review the definitions of elements and principles provided on pages 3–16. On a broader level, you might talk about materials artists use. Is it art if it isn't meant to last? Is the art the actual creation or the photo?

Acknowledgments

FEW ART TEACHERS are fortunate enough to work in an environment like Sycamore School. (I'm not sure there are other schools like Sycamore!) Certainly it would be hard to find a more supportive group of administrators, staff, faculty, and parents, and my students are the greatest! I thank all of those people—past and present—with whom I have worked and from whom I have learned.

Special thanks also go to:

Lauren Ditchley, my wonderful assistant, who helps me in countless ways. I simply could not do the job without her. She is a terrific teacher in her own right.

Betty Krebs and Courtney Henderson, the "fonts of all knowledge," without whose constant support none of us at Sycamore could teach or write books.

Larry Fletcher, John George, and B. J. Drewes, computer experts, who always figure out the problem.

Jerome Pohlen, my editor, for his encouragement and help.

Kelly Wilson, who had the unenviable task of finding all my mistakes.

Barbara Freeman, for being an outstanding friend for more than 40 years. She always helps me make my books easier to follow.

And as always, my terrific family: my wonderful husband, Irwin, for his humor and support, and my incredibly brilliant and talented sons, Ben and Josh (and Eric!), and the rest of the gang.

Bibliography

Anderson, Richard L. *Calliope's Sisters: A Comparative Study of Philosophies of Art.* Englewood Cliffs, NJ: Prentice-Hall, 1990.

Carle, Eric. *Hello, Red Fox.* New York: Aladdin, 2001.

Danto, Arthur C. *After the End of Art: Contemporary Art and the Pale of History.* Princeton, NJ: Princeton University Press, 1997.

Pink, Daniel H. *A Whole New Mind: Why Right-Brainers Will Rule the Future.* New York: Penguin, 2006.

Pinkwater, Daniel. *Fish Whistle.* Reading, MA: Addison-Wesley, 1989.

Prince, Eileen S. *Art Is Fundamental: Teaching the Elements and Principles of Art in Elementary School.* Chicago: Zephyr Press, 2008.

Prince, Eileen S. *Art Matters: Strategies, Ideas, and Activities to Strengthen Learning Across the Curriculum.* Chicago: Zephyr Press, 2002.

Index of Projects by Elements and Principles

IF YOU WOULD like to organize the activities in this book into more cohesive units, you might arrange many of them by the elements or principles they explore. Some, of course, focus on art history or theory, but most will relate to at least one element or principle. Almost all great works of art display balance and unity, so in those categories I have included only those projects that truly focus on those principles. (The same is true for value, which appears in virtually every piece of art in some way.) When the child is asked to create a work that expresses her feelings about some stimulus, any or all of the elements and principles might be involved. Once again, even if you do arrange these projects in some sort of unit, these activities do not represent a comprehensive curriculum. As you can see if you look at my book *Art Is Fundamental*, a complete curriculum builds from simple concepts to more complex ones and from skill to skill.

Below, I use the following key:

E = Everywhere
H = At Home
M = At the Art Museum
C = In the City
P = In the Park

Thus "M5" would refer to the fifth activity in the section "At the Art Museum." If the activity is in parentheses, this implies that the project includes the concept but that it is a secondary concern, not the main focus.

Elements

Line: E2, E3, E4, H5, H10, H16, C4, C5, C7, C9, possibly M4, P1, (P3), P6, P8, P9, P11

Shape: E3, E4, H2, H4, H20, (H23), C2, C4, C5, C7, C9, possibly M4, P1, (P3), (P4), P8, P9, P10

Color: E3, H1, H2, H4, H20, (H21), C5, C7, possibly M4, P1, P2, P3, P8, P9, P11

Value: E3, E4, H2, H6, H13, H15, (H19), C5, possibly M4, P1, P8, P9, P11

Texture: E3, E4, H2, (H6), H14, H19, C5, possibly M4, P1, P4, P8, P10

Form: H3, H8, (H16), H21, C2, C4, C5, possibly M4, P1, P4, P5, P10

Principles

Balance: E3, H4, H10, (H15), C5, possibly M4, P10
Contrast: E3, E4, H2, H6, H13, H19, C5, M4, possibly P11

Pattern: H1, H2, H14, H19, H20, C5, possibly M4, P11

Emphasis: (H6), (H11), (H15), (H18), (H20), (H22), (H23), (M5), (C9), (C10), (P5), (P7), (P9), (P11)

Unity: E3, C5, possibly M4

Repetition: H1, H2, H14, H19, H20, C5, possibly M4, P11

Movement: H5, H10 (H18), C5, possibly M4

Distortion: H4, H14, H17, H22, C5, possibly M4

Rhythm: E3, H2, H5, H18, C5, possibly M4

Simplification: H4, C9, possibly M4

Gradation: H7, H13, C5, possibly M4, P10

Art Matters

Strategies, Ideas, and Activities to Strengthen Learning Across the Curriculum

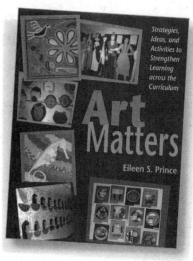

978-1-56976-129-8

$27.95 (CAN $41.95)

"Eileen Prince is a master teacher in every sense of the word. This book will be helpful to those who need good ideas for art units or projects, but it is far more than that. This approach is the foundation for development of a meaningful art curriculum for a school or district."

> —Virginia Burney, retired teacher and administrator

"*Art Matters* is a great how-to book for all teachers of any subject. It is well thought out, practical, and enables any teacher to integrate creative thinking and art experiences into the curriculum. Eileen Prince shows us that art is multidimensional and part of math, science, language arts, and social studies. Best of all, this book makes art realistic and fun."

> —Richard Cohen, retired teacher and board member, Magnet Schools Business Advisory Council, Indianapolis Public Schools